BRIDGING GRADES
3 to 4

Summer Bridge®
An imprint of Carson Dellosa Education
PO Box 35665
Greensboro, NC 27425 USA

© 2025 Carson Dellosa Education. Except as permitted under the United States Copyright Act, no part of this publication may be reproduced, stored, or distributed in any form or by any means (mechanically, electronically, recording, etc.) without the prior written consent of Carson Dellosa Education. Summer Bridge® is an imprint of Carson Dellosa Education.

Printed in the USA • All rights reserved.
ISBN 978-1-4838-7272-8
01-006251151

Caution: Exercise activities may require adult supervision. Before beginning any exercise activity, consult a physician. Written parental permission is suggested for those using this book in group situations. Children should always warm up prior to beginning any exercise activity and should stop immediately if they feel any discomfort during exercise.

Caution: Before beginning any food activity, ask parents' permission and inquire about the child's food allergies and religious or other food restrictions.

Caution: Nature activities may require adult supervision. Before beginning any nature activity, ask parents' permission and inquire about the child's plant and animal allergies. Remind the child not to touch plants or animals during the activity without adult supervision.

Caution: Before completing any balloon activity, ask parents' permission and inquire about possible latex allergies. Also, remember that uninflated or popped balloons may present a choking hazard. The authors and publisher are not responsible or liable for any injury that may result from performing the exercises or activities in this book.

Table of Contents

How to Use Your *Summer Bridge Activities®* Book 4
Skills Matrix 6
Summer Reading and Free E-books 8
Section 1: Monthly Goals and Word List 10
Introduction to Flexibility 11
Let's Play Today Activities 12
Activity Pages 13
Science Experiments 53
Social Studies Activities 55
Section 2: Monthly Goals and Word List 58
Introduction to Strength 59
Let's Play Today Activities 60
Activity Pages 61
Science Experiments 101
Social Studies Activities 103
Section 3: Monthly Goals and Word List 106
Introduction to Endurance 107
Let's Play Today Activities 108
Activity Pages 109
Science Experiments 149
Social Studies Activities 151
Reflect and Reset 154
Answer Key 156
Flash Cards
Progress Chart
Reference Chart

How to Use Your *Summer Bridge Activities*® Book

Three Summer Months, 15 Minutes a Day

The three color-coded sections match the three months of summer. Your child has two pages to complete each weekday (a front and a back), taking about 15 minutes total. The activities are designed to reinforce third-grade skills and introduce fourth-grade topics.

Special Features

Summer Reading Fun:
free e-books, a reading log, and ideas to make reading fun

Charts and Poster:
a helpful fact reference chart, a progress chart with stickers, and a summer bucket list poster

Science and Social Studies Activities:
monthly hands-on science experiments and interesting social studies activities

Flash Cards:
tear-out flash cards for hands-on practice

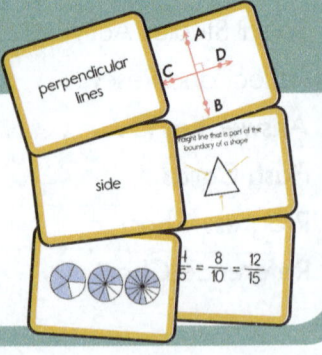

Healthy Habits Sidebars

Mindful Moments

activities focused on social and emotional learning

Let's Play Today

activities encouraging physical activity and play

Fast Fun Facts

fun trivia facts that inspire a love of learning

© Carson Dellosa Education

The adventure continues online with IXL!

Throughout this edition of Summer Bridge Activities®, you'll see 3-digit codes that connect your family with fun, motivating online practice questions on IXL, the most widely used K-12 online learning program in the U.S. On IXL.com or the IXL mobile app, simply type the 3-digit code into the Skill ID box to start "playing" IXL and earning fun awards and certificates!

Try IXL free with 10 questions per day, and learn about how an IXL membership can boost learning even further. With an IXL account you'll get:

Limitless learning
Boost learning and curiosity with over 17,000 topics in math, English, science, social studies, and Spanish for everyone, from K-12.

Support and encouragement
Get instant feedback, step-by-step explanations, videos, and more! IXL makes it easy to learn from mistakes and feel good about it.

Awards and certificates
Whimsical awards and certificates celebrate your child's achievements and keep them motivated.

A unique plan for every child
IXL builds a growth path for your child by meeting them at their learning level and giving them exactly what they need to work on next.

The learning app families trust
In over 75 scientific research studies, IXL is proven to help students make bigger learning gains and build confidence in their abilities. No wonder it's used by 1 in 4 students across the U.S.!

Ready to open up an exciting new world of learning?

Join hundreds of thousands of parents across the world and give your child access to unlimited learning with an IXL membership!

Learn more at
ixl.com/summer-bridge/3-4

Skills Matrix

Day	Addition & Subtraction	Fractions	Geometry	Graphing & Probability	Language Arts & Writing	Measurement	Multiplication & Division	Numbers	Parts of Speech	Place Value	Prefixes & Suffixes	Problem Solving	Punctuation & Capitalization	Reading Comprehension	Science	Sentence Structure	Social Studies	Spelling	Vocabulary	Word Study
1												★		★					★	
2							★	★					★							★
3	★				★		★					★								
4				★	★				★			★								
5							★		★					★						
6							★						★							
7				★					★	★						★				
8						★								★						
9						★								★						
10		★	★						★							★				
11							★		★										★	
12							★						★							
13							★							★						★
14		★			★	★														
15		★							★			★							★	
16					★				★			★								
17							★							★						
18					★		★		★											
19					★		★							★						
20	★						★	★												
BONUS PAGES!															★		★			
1					★		★					★								
2					★				★					★					★	
3									★	★								★		
4			★		★														★	
5	★		★		★		★													
6							★		★										★	
7	★				★		★									★				
8					★		★							★						
9							★							★				★		
10	★						★			★									★	
11	★				★					★									★	

Skills Matrix

Day	Addition & Subtraction	Fractions	Geometry	Graphing & Probability	Language Arts & Writing	Measurement	Multiplication & Division	Numbers	Parts of Speech	Place Value	Prefixes & Suffixes	Problem Solving	Punctuation & Capitalization	Reading Comprehension	Science	Sentence Structure	Social Studies	Spelling	Vocabulary	Word Study
12		★								★			★	★						
13		★						★						★						
14		★		★	★					★										
15					★							★								
16					★								★	★						
17		★				★							★	★						
18		★							★									★		
19	★	★					★												★	★
20		★												★				★		
					BONUS PAGES!										★		★			
1	★						★							★				★		
2						★								★						
3					★									★						
4					★	★	★	★												
5		★								★				★						
6		★												★					★	
7		★			★	★								★						
8			★											★						★
9			★					★		★										
10		★			★									★						
11	★				★															
12					★	★								★						
13		★			★														★	★
14		★											★	★						
15								★						★		★				
16	★				★					★				★						
17	★	★												★		★				
18					★								★	★						
19			★		★									★						
20	★									★				★						
					BONUS PAGES!										★		★			

Summer Reading and Free E-books

Reading is important all year, not just during school. This summer, set yourself a reading goal and challenge yourself to complete it. You can make your goal one book a month, or even one a week! Choose a goal realistic for you.

Give some of these summer reading ideas a try to make summer reading fun and meaningful.

Read in a New Place

Read in a hammock, under a shady tree, in a sunny spot, on a porch, in a park, in a fort, on a picnic blanket, at a playground, in a tent, or any other spot you've never read before.

Make a Reading List

Make a list of books in a genre you like, books with characters your age, books by your favorite author, or come up with your own list theme. Read as many as you can and check them off as you do.

Read a Summer Book

Choose a book that is summer themed. It could be about a summer trip, summer vacation, a new neighbor, a fun adventure, or set at the beach or in a tropical location.

Be a Chef

Read a cookbook or a book about food. Choose a recipe in the book to make. Write it on a recipe card. Then make it (and enjoy it)! It's up to you if you share it!

Check Your Library

Sign up for your local library's summer reading challenge (or find one online to participate in).

Start a Book Club

Join (or start) a book club with friends or family members. Take turns choosing the book.

Free E-books!

Get started on summer reading fun now by scanning the QR codes for free e-books!

Animal Abilities

Mega-Cool Megafauna: Creatures of Ancient Seas

Jayla Cole, Queen of the Goal

Pura Belpré

SUMMER READING LOG

DATE	TITLE	Minutes Read	# OF PAGES

SECTION 1

Monthly Goals

A goal is something that you want to accomplish. Sometimes, reaching a goal can be hard work!

Think of three goals to set for yourself this month. For example, you may want to read for 30 minutes each day. Write your goals on the lines and review them with an adult.

Place a sticker next to each of your goals that you complete. Feel proud that you have met your goals!

1. _____   PLACE STICKER

2. _____   PLACE STICKER

3. _____   PLACE STICKER

Word List

The following words are used in this section. Read each word. Use a dictionary to look up each word that you do not know. Write two sentences. Use a word from the word list in each sentence.

briefly	exhibition
bronze	glacier
concentrate	league
design	receive
displayed	representing

4. _____

5. _____

10 © Carson Dellosa Education

Introduction to Flexibility

This section includes Let's Play Today and Mindful Moments activities that focus on flexibility. These activities are designed to help you become flexible physically and mentally. If you have limited mobility, feel free to modify any suggested activity or choose a different one from the list on the following page.

When we talk about flexibility with regard to our bodies, we are referring to how easily our bodies move. If our body isn't flexible, then we will have trouble doing everyday tasks, such as tying our shoes, reaching for things, or playing games or sports.

Over the summer, make a point to stretch regularly to keep your arms and legs moving easily and your back from getting sore. Challenge yourself to touch your toes daily. Did you know that everyday activities, like reaching for a dropped pencil, can help you practice stretching?

Mental flexibility is just as important as physical flexibility. Being mentally flexible means being open-minded. We all know how disappointing it can be when things do not go the way we want them to. Having a fun day at the park ruined because of rain is frustrating. Feeling disappointed or angry as a reaction is normal. In life, there will be situations where unexpected things happen. Often, it is how someone reacts to those circumstances that affects the outcome. It is important to have realistic expectations, brainstorm solutions to improve a disappointing situation, or look on the bright side of a disappointment to find joy even when things do not go as planned.

You can show flexibility of character and mind by being understanding, respecting others' differences, sharing, taking turns, and more. Learning to be flexible now at your age will give you the ability to handle unexpected situations in the years to come.

Engaging Online Practice

Bring learning to life with fun, interactive activities on IXL! Look for the Skill ID box and type the 3-digit code into the search bar on IXL.com or the IXL mobile app. Ten questions per day are free!

Skill IDs: 5UN • D9K

SECTION 1

Let's Play Today

Get up and moving with these Let's Play Today activities. Section 1 focuses on flexibility. Flexibility helps your body move in its full range of motion and helps you avoid injuring yourself when exercising or playing. Use this list in addition to or as a replacement for any Let's Play Today suggestions on the activity pages. This list was developed to be inclusive of a variety of abilities. Choose the ones that are a good fit for you! Make modifications as needed. These activities may require adult supervision. See page 2 for full caution information.

Bouncy Ball Back-and-Forth:

In an open outdoor space, kick or toss a large bouncy ball back and forth with a friend, family member, or neighbor. Stretch your legs when you kick the ball or lunge to stop a returning ball. Stretch your arms if you are catching it.

The Shallow End Hop:

In the shallow end of a pool, stand on one leg and hold your arms out to your side. Hop from one side of the pool to the other without using your other leg. Switch legs and hop back to the other side.

Stretch to Pop:

Grab a container of bubbles and head outside. Blow bubbles high into the air. Stretch your arms and legs to reach them and pop them before they fall back toward the ground.

Walk a Tightrope:

Use a piece of sidewalk chalk or tape to make a long, thin line on the cement outside. Putting one foot in front of the other and with arms stretched out to the side, slowly walk on the line until you come to the end, being careful to keep your balance. Then turn around and walk back the other way. Try not to step off the line.

Weaving In and Out:

In a yard or at a playground, set up an obstacle course that is made up of traffic cones, toys, or other objects. Start with the objects spread out pretty far, and then move them closer together to make it a little more difficult. Try to move through it without touching any of the objects.

© Carson Dellosa Education

Problem Solving/Vocabulary

Solve each word problem.

1. Yoshiro is picking apples. He puts 36 apples in each box. How many apples does he put in 9 boxes?

   He puts 4 in each box

2. Miss Brown has 25 students in her class. She wants to make 5 equal teams for a relay race. How many students will be on each team?

3. Andre has saved $9.00 toward buying a new ball. He will get $3.00 today from his father. How much more money will he need to buy the $19.95 ball?

4. Samaria saves 867 pennies in May, 942 in June, and 716 in July. How much money does she save in these three months?

Read each group of related words. Write two more related words for each group.

5. robin, owl, pigeon — quail — wren

6. peaches, apples, pears — _____ — _____

7. spoon, bowl, cup — _____ — _____

8. lake, pond, river — _____ — _____

9. dollar, dime, penny — _____ — _____

10. dress, shoes, skirt — _____ — _____

Read the passage. Then, answer the questions.

Glaciers

A glacier is a large, thick mass of ice. It forms when snow hardens into ice over a long period of time. It might not look like it, but glaciers can move. Glaciers usually move slowly. If a lot of ice melts at once, a glacier may **surge** forward, or move suddenly. Most glaciers are found in Antarctica (the continent at the South Pole) or in Greenland (a country near the North Pole). Areas with glaciers receive a lot of snowfall in the winter and have cool summers. Most glaciers are located in the mountains where few people live. Occasionally, glaciers can cause flooding in cities and towns. Falling ice from glaciers may block the path of people hiking on trails farther down the mountain. Icebergs are large, floating pieces of ice that have broken off from glaciers. Icebergs can cause problems for ships at sea.

11. What is the main idea of this passage?

   A. Icebergs can be dangerous to ships.

   B. Glaciers are large masses of ice found mainly in the mountains.

   C. People usually live far away from glaciers.

12. How does a glacier form? _____

   _____

13. What does the word *surge* mean in this passage?

   A. move forward suddenly

   B. freeze into ice

   C. break off from an iceberg

14. Where are most glaciers located? _____

15. What is the weather like where glaciers are found? _____

   _____

Mindful Moment

Breathe in counting to three. Breathe out counting to three. Do this five times.

14 © Carson Dellosa Education

Word Study/Numbers

DAY 2

Write the base word of each word.

1. playful _____
2. disinterest _____
3. rewrite _____
4. uncover _____
5. spoonful _____
6. quickly _____
7. happiness _____
8. doubtful _____

Follow the directions.

9. Draw a square around the greatest number.

10. Count by twos to 40. Underline the numbers you use in order.

11. Draw a triangle around the number that is 4 less than 62.

12. Draw an X over each odd number.

13. Circle all of the capital letters. Write the letters you circled in order, starting with the top row and moving left to right.

_____

b	r	q	e	o	S	c	r	y	10	6	3
U	y	10	5	2	4	M	z	1	q	a	i
6	v	0	7	8	M	p	2	10	17	12	l
r	b	14	18	b	e	16	f	h	19	E	s
18	5	14	7	2	p	m	n	z	58	20	s
94	86	22	2	R	17	I	0	24	n	x	c
26	39	3	a	d	e	28	g	S	52	19	30
7	j	F	k	32	y	34	4	31	t	10	36
0	n	e	n	38	o	80	98	U	47	x	p
w	m	m	11	N	3	14	39	c	r	e	t
q	u	v	9	7	6	w	5	40	w	13	19

© Carson Dellosa Education

15

Multiplication & Division/Capitalization

Use the fact family in each circle to make number sentences.

14.

15.

16.

___ × ___ = ___   ___ × ___ = ___   ___ × ___ = ___

___ × ___ = ___   ___ × ___ = ___   ___ × ___ = ___

___ ÷ ___ = ___   ___ ÷ ___ = ___   ___ ÷ ___ = ___

___ ÷ ___ = ___   ___ ÷ ___ = ___   ___ ÷ ___ = ___

Each important word in a title should begin with a capital letter. Read the sentences. Draw three short lines under each letter that should be a capital, like this: c̲.

17. On the way to Grandma's, we listened to the audiobook *One crazy summer*.

18. Dad gets a little teary when he hears the Beatles song "let it Be."

19. This year, the high school is putting on the musical *into the Woods*.

20. If you like mysteries, read *Watcher in the piney woods*.

21. At Ruby's sleepover, we watched *how to train your dragon*.

22. Zarie memorized Maya Angelou's poem "life doesn't frighten me."

23. My sister and I have watched the movie *frozen* four times.

© Carson Dellosa Education

Addition/Language Arts

Skill IDs: 9NH • 74E

DAY 3

Add to find each sum.

1. 634
   + 68

2.   87
   + 89

3. 888
   + 45

4. 732
   + 99

5. 496
   + 94

6. 557
   + 23

7. 347
   + 54

8. 665
   + 37

Rewrite each set of underlined words to make it a possessive.

9. Have you seen the mitten belonging to Margot?

   _____

10. We put the bike belonging to Salim in the garage.

    _____

11. The chirping of the birds woke me up.

    _____

12. Lauren lost the goggles belonging to Mariko in the pool.

    _____

 **Let's Play Today** *See page 12.

Do the mountain pose: put your feet shoulder's width apart, bend your knees slightly, put your arms at your side with your palms out, and stand up straight.

© Carson Dellosa Education

17

DAY 3

Prefixes/Multiplication

Read the story. Then, write the correct prefix in each blank. Use *dis-*, *in-*, *re-*, or *un-*.

My uncle Paul worked in a bookstore. Uncle Paul always helped me find books to read. He was never (13.) _____ pleased if I asked him for help. I (14.) _____ call the day I asked for a book about unsolved mysteries. Uncle Paul (15.) _____ covered some on the very top of the back shelf. They were dirty and smelled dusty. They looked as if they had been (16.) _____ touched for years.

I started to read one. As I looked (17.) _____ side, I noticed that some of the pages were missing from the very end of the book. "Oh, no!" I said. "This story is (18.) _____ complete. Now, I'll never know how it ends." I must have looked pretty (19.) _____ appointed because Uncle Paul tried to cheer me up. He said, "I think you (20.) _____ covered a real unsolved mystery!"

Choose three words with prefixes from the story. Write the words and their meanings on the lines.

_____

_____

_____

21. 30
    × 9

22. 50
    × 5

23. 80
    × 3

24. 90
    × 7

Problem Solving/Language Arts

Solve each word problem.

1. I read 6 books each month in June, July, and August. How many books did I read during these three months?

2. Carla went on a trip. She took 120 photos during her 3-day trip. How many photos did she take each day?

3. Josie observed birds in her backyard for one week. She saw 6 birds each day. How many birds did she see in all?

4. Nico had a sleepover and invited 7 friends. His stepmom made 32 mini muffins for breakfast. How many muffins could each boy have?

Underline the word that correctly completes each sentence.

5. Luis and Kate (is, are) looking for something to do on a sunny day.

6. They decide to (makes, make) an obstacle course.

7. Kate drags out a few old tires that (her, she) dad said were in the garage.

8. Luis (brings, bring) over three pool noodles.

9. After a lot of work, Kate and Luis are satisfied with (our, their) obstacle course.

10. "Who should (try, tries) it first?" asks Kate.

Study the pictograph. Then, answer each question.

Month	Tires Sold
Jan.	⭕⭕⭕⭕⭕◐
Feb.	⭕⭕
March	⭕◐
April	⭕⭕⭕◐
May	⭕

Key	⭕ = 500 tires

11. How many more tires were sold in April than in February?

_____

12. What is the difference between the least number of tires sold in a month and the greatest number of tires sold in a month?

_____

An adjective is a word that describes a noun. Circle the adjective that describes each underlined noun.

13. Some prairie dogs live in large <u>communities</u> underground.

14. A mother prairie dog makes a nest of dried <u>plants</u> in the spring.

15. She gives birth to a litter of four <u>pups</u>.

16. She is a good <u>mother</u> and takes care of her pups.

17. The pups are ready to venture outside after six <u>weeks</u>.

18. The pups have many <u>friends</u>.

Reading Comprehension

Read the passage. Then, answer the questions.

The Olympic Games

During the Olympic Games, people from all over the world gather to compete in different sporting events. The original Olympics were held in Greece around 776 BCE. Athletes came together every four years to run races of different lengths. Those who won were given wreaths of olive branches. The modern Olympics were first held in 1896 in Greece. In 1994, the International Olympic Committee decided that the summer and winter Olympic Games should be held in different years. This means that every two years, thousands of people **representing** more than 200 countries come together to compete in either summer or winter sports. Today's top athletes receive gold, silver, or bronze medals and compete in hundreds of different events. The Olympics give each host country a chance to show its culture both to the people who come there and to the people who watch on TV. The sports may be different than in the original Olympics, but the spirit of goodwill and good sportsmanship is still the same.

1. What is the main idea of this passage?

   A. The Olympics are held every four years.

   B. People come to the Olympics from all over the world to compete.

   C. Today's top athletes receive gold, silver, or bronze medals.

2. When and where were the original Olympics held? _____

3. How did the Olympics change in 1994? _____

   _____

4. What does the word *representing* mean? _____

   _____

5. How do the Olympics help people learn about different cultures? _____

   _____

© Carson Dellosa Education

21

DAY 5

Multiplication/Parts of Speech

Skill IDs: YPF • 5LM
Search for these skill IDs on IXL.com for more practice!

Find the value of ? in each problem below.

6. 6 × (5 × ?) = (6 × 5) × 12   ? = _____

7. (? × 9) × 3 = 16 × (9 × 3)   ? = _____

8. (5 × 8) × 10 = 5 × (? × 10)   ? = _____

9. 2 × (? × 6) = (2 × 14) × 6   ? = _____

10. (? × 6) × 11 = 9 × (6 × 11)   ? = _____

11. 20 × (4 × 7) = (? × 4) × 7   ? = _____

Write the correct forms of each adjective.

		Adjectives That Compare Two Nouns	Adjectives That Compare More Than Two Nouns
12.	long	longer	longest
13.	soft	_____	_____
14.	large	_____	_____
15.	flat	_____	_____
16.	sweet	_____	_____

Fast Fun Fact

Question marks didn't always look the way they do now. They used to look more like a tilde (~).

Multiplication & Division

Multiply.

1. 4 × 12 = _____
2. 11 × 9 = _____
3. 6 × 11 = _____

4. 9 × 6 = _____
5. 5 × 6 = _____
6. 9 × 2 = _____

7. 10 × 3 = _____
8. 7 × 7 = _____
9. 8 × 9 = _____

Divide.

10. 22 ÷ 2 = _____
11. 25 ÷ 5 = _____
12. 28 ÷ 4 = _____

13. 14 ÷ 7 = _____
14. 36 ÷ 6 = _____
15. 18 ÷ 3 = _____

16. 81 ÷ 9 = _____
17. 33 ÷ 3 = _____
18. 64 ÷ 8 = _____

Mindful Moment

Think of a time when you did something nice for a friend or family member. How did this make you feel?

DAY 6

Problem Solving/Parts of Speech

Solve each word problem. Show your work.

19. Wei made 8 quarts of punch for the party. How many cups did he make?

20. Together, two boxes of spices weigh 4 pounds 8 ounces. Each pound is worth $400. How much are the boxes worth in all?

21. Mr. Rivera gave each student in his class a calculator. Each calculator weighed 16 ounces. If Mr. Rivera gave each of his 20 students a calculator, how many pounds did the calculators weigh in all?

22. Corbin's school ordered 20 boxes of milk. In each box, there were 35 containers of milk. By the end of the week, 265 containers were used. How many containers were left?

A noun names a person, a place, or a thing. An action verb tells what a noun is doing. Circle the nouns. Underline the verbs.

elephant	sang	ate	fixed
laugh	tent	Mr. Chip	team
book	California	guitar	landed
Lake Street	cleaned	yell	played

Parts of Speech/Graphing

DAY 7

Abstract nouns are feelings, concepts, and ideas. Some examples are *hope*, *bravery*, and *pride*. Underline the abstract noun in each sentence.

1. Colonel Graham knows that the cadets have respect for her.

2. We could see Izzy's satisfaction when she finally finished the puzzle.

3. Ryan's silliness made the whole group laugh.

4. Dionne showed courage when he faced the auditorium and started to speak.

Study the bar graph. Then, answer each question.

5. What is the total number of students who like social studies?

_____

6. How many total students are in third grade? Fourth grade?

_____ _____

7. Which subjects have the greatest difference between third and fourth grade?

_____ _____

8. How many more students like math than reading in third grade? Fourth grade?

_____ _____

© Carson Dellosa Education

25

Round each number to the nearest 10.

9. 28 = _____   10. 85 = _____   11. 13 = _____   12. 44 = _____

Round each number to the nearest 100.

13. 767 = _____   14. 841 = _____   15. 211 = _____   16. 587 = _____

Read each sentence. On the line, write *S* if it is a simple sentence, *C* if it is a compound sentence, and *CX* if it is a complex sentence. Then, underline each conjunction in the compound and complex sentences.

17. _____ Before school starts, Jada wants a new backpack.

18. _____ Mr. O'Rourke retired from teaching last year.

19. _____ Unless you finish your homework, we won't be able to watch the movie.

20. _____ Owen and Rosie are going camping today, but they'll be back on Sunday.

21. _____ We can cook chicken, or we can go out for dinner.

22. _____ Although I like to ride my bike, I'm going to roller-skate to Jenna's house today.

23. _____ Nazim is going to vacuum, and Molly is going to dust.

24. _____ Because Gabriela lost the book, she'll have to pay a fine.

Measurement/Punctuation  DAY 8

Jonah and his mom are building a raised garden bed. Jonah measures the boards he finds in the shed that might be useful. Draw an X above the line plot to show the length of each board.

$42\frac{1}{2}$ inches	$46\frac{3}{4}$ inches
42 inches	$40\frac{1}{4}$ inches
$46\frac{3}{4}$ inches	$42\frac{1}{2}$ inches
$40\frac{1}{4}$ inches	$40\frac{1}{4}$ inches
$42\frac{1}{2}$ inches	$40\frac{1}{4}$ inches
$46\frac{3}{4}$ inches	44 inches

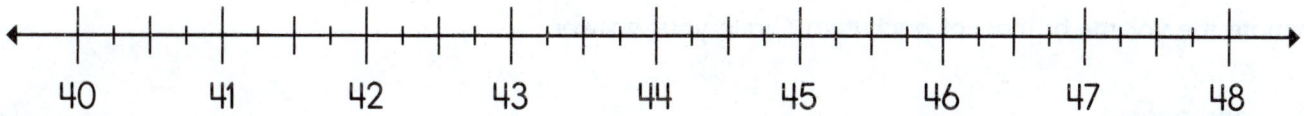

To add commas where they are needed in the dialogue below, use a mark like this: ⌃.

1. "I'd like to ride the Ferris wheel first" said Anya.

2. "The fair seems even more crowded this year than last" commented Riley.

3. "I can't go on anything that spins" said Kahlil "because it makes me feel sick."

4. Anya asked "What time are you meeting your parents?"

5. "The line is too long for the rocket ship ride" decided Riley.

 *See page 12.

Touch your toes 10 times.

© Carson Dellosa Education   27

DAY 8

Measurement

Find the area of each figure.

6.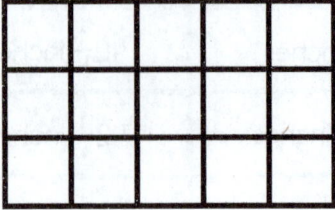

_____ × _____ = _____
base   height   total area

7.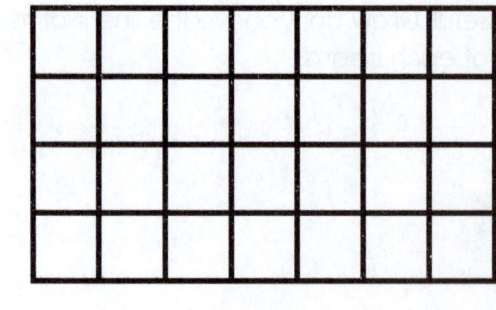

_____ × _____ = _____
base   height   total area

Estimate the volume or mass of each item. Circle your answer.

8. one peanut

    A. 1 gram   **B.** 100 grams   **C.** 1 kilogram

9. the amount of liquid in one teaspoon

    A. 5 milliliters   **B.** 50 milliliters   **C.** 500 milliliters

10. the amount of liquid a bathtub can hold

    A. 1 liter   **B.** 150 liters   **C.** 15 milliliters

Solve the word problem.

11. The DeMarco family is moving. Their largest box weighs 50 kilograms. It has a mass 5 times greater than the mass of their smallest box. What is the mass of their smallest box? _____

Measurement

Write the perimeter of each figure or the missing side lengths.

1.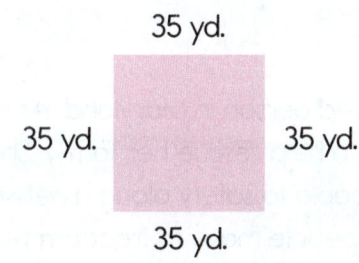

   perimeter = _____ yd.

2.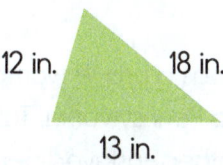

   perimeter = _____ in.

3.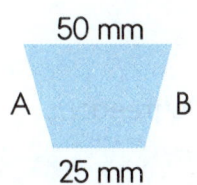

   perimeter = 235 mm

   Side A = _____ mm   Side B = _____ mm

4.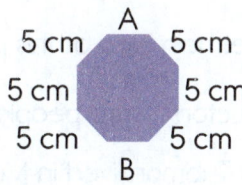

   perimeter = 40 cm

   Side A = _____ cm   Side B = _____ cm

Solve the problems.

5. Mr. Wen needs to replace a section of fence that measures 3 feet by 17 feet. What is the area of the fence that needs to be replaced?

6. Alysha wants to frame a drawing she made. It measures 8 inches by 12 inches. What is the area of the frame she needs?

Search for this skill ID on IXL.com for more practice!

Reading Comprehension

Read the passage. Then, answer the questions.

Harriet Tubman

Harriet Tubman was a brave woman. She grew up as an enslaved person in Maryland. As an adult, she escaped north to Pennsylvania. Tubman returned to Maryland to help rescue her family. She returned many times to help other enslaved people. She guided enslaved people to safety along a network known as the Underground Railroad. People who helped enslaved people move to freedom were called "conductors." They were named after the people who manage trains and their crews on railroads. In 1861, the United States began fighting the Civil War. This war was a struggle between northern and southern states, mainly about whether people should be enslaved. President Abraham Lincoln signed a law in 1863. The law stated that slavery was no longer allowed in the United States. With the law on her side, Tubman continued for many years to help people who were treated unfairly.

7. What is the main idea of this passage?

   A. "Conductors" were people who helped enslaved people move to freedom.

   B. Harriet Tubman lived in Maryland.

   C. Harriet Tubman helped people on the Underground Railroad.

8. Why did Tubman return to Maryland? _____

   _____

9. What was the Underground Railroad? _____

   _____

10. What did conductors on the Underground Railroad do? _____

    _____

11. What was the Civil War? _____

    _____

Fractions/Sentence Structure

Draw a line between fractions that are equivalent, or equal.

$\frac{3}{6}$ $\frac{2}{8}$

$\frac{2}{3}$ $\frac{1}{2}$

$\frac{3}{3}$ $\frac{4}{6}$

$\frac{1}{4}$ 1

Combine each pair of simple sentences to write compound sentences. Use the conjunction shown in parentheses ( ). Do not forget to write a comma before the conjunction in each sentence.

1. We might go to the park. We might go to the store. (or)

   We might go to the park, or we might go to the store.

2. My dog is ready to play. My cat wants to nap. (but)

   _____

   _____

3. It may rain tonight. The party will be indoors. (so)

   _____

   _____

DAY 10

Skill IDs P87 • F6X

Geometry/Parts of Speech

Label each shape with letters from the box that describe it.

| A = quadrilateral | B = parallelogram | C = rhombus | D = polygon |

4.
   _____

5.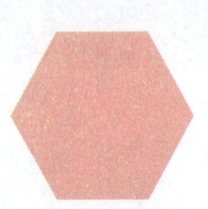
   _____

6.
   _____

7.
   _____

8.
   _____

9.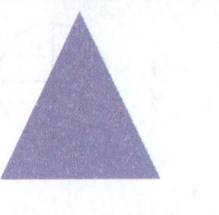
   _____

A possessive pronoun is a pronoun that shows ownership. Some possessive pronouns include:

| mine | ours | your | his | hers | their | its | my | our |

Write two sentences. Use a possessive pronoun in each sentence.

10. _____

_____

11. _____

_____

Fast Fun Fact

The triangle is the strongest shape. That is why you will see it used to build bridges, buildings, ships, and more!

32 © Carson Dellosa Education

Vocabulary

Write the word from the word bank that matches each description.

| knead | sense | praise | certain |
| wheat | purchase | numb | guide |

1. unable to feel _____

2. we do this to dough _____

3. sure of something _____

4. to buy something _____

5. to see, hear, feel, taste, or smell _____

6. flour is made from this _____

7. a leader of a group _____

8. to express approval _____

Circle the word that fits each definition.

9. (hour, our): a unit of time made up of 60 minutes

10. (knew, new): not worn or used

11. (here, hear): to take in sound through your ears

DAY 11

Division/Parts of Speech

Divide to find each quotient.

12. $3\overline{)18}$ 13. $4\overline{)24}$ 14. $3\overline{)21}$ 15. $4\overline{)36}$

16. $5\overline{)40}$ 17. $6\overline{)36}$ 18. $8\overline{)40}$ 19. $9\overline{)27}$

Write an adjective in each blank to complete each sentence.

20. The bear has _____ , _____ fur.

21. The _____ birds woke me up this morning.

22. Her _____ , _____ balloon floated away.

Demonstrative adjectives identify specific people, places, or things. Write the correct demonstrative adjective (*this*, *that*, *these*, or *those*) to complete each sentence. Use *this* and *that* with singular nouns. Use *these* and *those* with plural nouns.

23. _____ book is one of my favorites.

24. _____ planet is very far away.

25. _____ ducks didn't come back to the pond this year.

Mindful Moment

Change the steps in your morning routine. For example, if you normally eat breakfast and then get dressed, get dressed first one day.

Division/Punctuation

Divide each set of objects into the correct number of groups.

1. Make 3 equal groups.

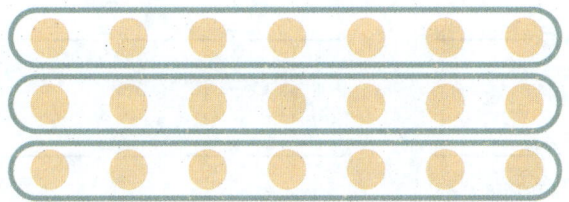

How many are in each group? __7__

2. Make 5 equal groups.

How many are in each group? _____

3. Make 2 equal groups.

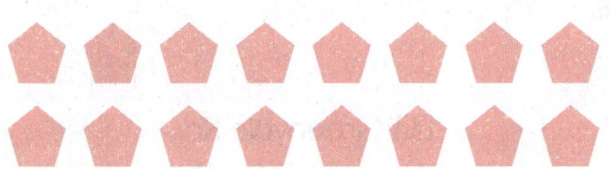

How many are in each group? _____

4. Make 4 equal groups.

How many are in each group? _____

Add commas where they belong in each sentence.

5. August 10, 1989, and May 10, 1985, are birth dates in our family.

6. My mom and stepdad were married in Portland Oregon on May 1 2011.

7. We had sushi salad soup and ice cream for dinner.

8. George Washington became the first US president on April 30 1789.

9. We saw deer bears elk and goats on our trip.

DAY 12

Skill IDs: XSK • UHF

Multiplication & Division/Punctuation

Complete each fact family.

10. 5 × 3 = ____

____ × ____ = ____

____ ÷ ____ = ____

____ ÷ ____ = ____

11. 21 ÷ 3 = ____

____ ÷ ____ = ____

____ × ____ = ____

____ × ____ = ____

12. 30 ÷ 6 = ____

____ ÷ ____ = ____

____ × ____ = ____

____ × ____ = ____

Add the missing commas to each address below. Use this symbol to add them: ⁏ .

13.

19052 Tanglewood Dr.
Rocky River OH 44116

14.

958 East Oak Lane #17
Baltimore MD 21218

15.

35 Frog Creek Woods
Harrisburg PA 17111

16.

133 Greenvale Rd.
Lincoln NE 68516

17.

21896 Sardis Court
Portland OR 97215

18.

568 Elm Street
Colton CA 92324

Multiplication/Word Study

Use the distributive property to make the problems easier to solve.

1. 8 × 16 =

   (8 × __10__) + (8 × __6__) = __128__

2. 9 × 15 =

   (9 × _____) + (9 × _____) = _____

3. 18 × 6 =

   (_____ × 6) + (_____ × 6) = _____

4. 20 × 12 =

   (20 × _____) + (20 × _____) = _____

5. 14 × 8 =

   (_____ × 8) + (_____ × 8) = _____

6. 8 × 22 =

   (8 × _____) + (8 × _____) = _____

Write the correct word from the word bank to answer each question.

| night | different | hopped | baby | knock |

7. Which word begins with a silent letter? _____

8. Which word does not end with a letter *t* but does end with a t sound?
   _____

9. Which word has a silent *gh*? _____

10. Which word has the *long e* sound, but does not include the letter *e*?
    _____

11. Which word has three syllables? _____

Roberto Clemente

Roberto Clemente was born in Puerto Rico in 1934. He played baseball in his neighborhood as a child. Then, he played for his high school team. He joined a junior national league when he was 16. He played baseball briefly in Canada before signing to play for the Pittsburgh Pirates in 1954. Clemente served in the US Marine Reserves for several years. That helped him grow stronger physically. He helped the Pirates win two World Series. During the off-season, Clemente often went back to Puerto Rico to help people. He liked visiting children in hospitals to give them hope that they could get well. An earthquake hit the country of Nicaragua in 1972. At age 38, Clemente died in an airplane crash on his way to deliver supplies to Nicaragua. He was elected to the Baseball Hall of Fame in 1973. He was the first Latino player to receive that honor.

12. What is the main idea of this passage?

    A. Roberto Clemente was a great baseball player who also helped people.

    B. Roberto Clemente died in an airplane crash.

    C. Roberto Clemente was elected to the Baseball Hall of Fame.

13. Where was Clemente born? _____

14. Where in the United States did Clemente play baseball? _____

15. What did Clemente do during the off-season? _____

16. Why was Clemente flying to Nicaragua? _____

Let's Play Today *See page 12.

Play a game you know well, but change a rule or two. For example, you could play hide-and-seek, but every time the seeker finds a player, the player becomes the new seeker.

Fractions/Language Arts

Compare the fractions. Use the greater than (>), less than (<), or equal to (=) symbols.

1. $\frac{1}{6}$ ◯ $\frac{1}{10}$
2. $\frac{2}{4}$ ◯ $\frac{2}{8}$
3. $\frac{3}{5}$ ◯ $\frac{4}{5}$

4. $\frac{2}{6}$ ◯ $\frac{4}{6}$
5. $\frac{3}{10}$ ◯ $\frac{3}{4}$
6. $\frac{4}{5}$ ◯ $\frac{4}{10}$

7. $\frac{5}{9}$ ◯ $\frac{2}{9}$
8. $\frac{6}{12}$ ◯ $\frac{1}{12}$
9. $\frac{3}{4}$ ◯ $\frac{1}{2}$

An idiom is a word or phrase that cannot be taken literally. Read each sentence below. Then, write the meaning of the underlined idiom.

10. Before Kayla went onstage last night, her parents gave her a kiss and told her to break a leg.

    _____

11. Jorge is feeling under the weather, so he's going to stay home from school.

    _____

12. Grandpa has a wonderful vegetable garden—he has quite a green thumb!

    _____

13. Mom said that a new transmission for the car will cost an arm and a leg.

    _____

Fractions/Measurement

Draw lines to divide each shape according to the fraction given.

14. fourths

15. eighths

16. halves

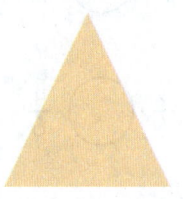

Write the time shown on each clock.

17. _____ : _____

18. _____ : _____

19. _____ : _____

20. _____ : _____

21. _____ : _____

22. _____ : _____

Problem Solving/Vocabulary

Solve each word problem.

1. Today's high was 86°. Yesterday, it was 9° colder. Two days ago, it was 6° colder than yesterday. What was the high temperature two days ago?

2. Annabel is 53 inches tall. Nicholas is 4 feet 4 inches tall. How many inches taller is Annabel?

3. Terrell brought 42 muffins to school for his birthday. He gave one each to the 17 students in his class and to the 19 students in the other third-grade class. How many extra muffins did he have?

4. Natasha can ride her bike at a rate of 10 miles per hour. How many miles can she go if she rides from 10:00 a.m. to 3:00 p.m.?

Circle the word that does not belong in each group of words. Then, describe why the other words belong together.

5. tuba, clarinet, jazz, flute, harp _____

6. tire, hammer, screwdriver, wrench _____

7. robin, hawk, sparrow, dog, crow _____

8. Moon, Mars, Earth, Jupiter, Venus _____

9. rose, daisy, lazy, tulip, lily _____

DAY 15

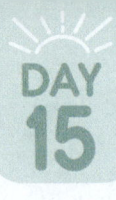

Fractions/Parts of Speech

Skill IDs: 7QM • CSP
Search for these skill IDs on IXL.com for more practice!

Mark each fraction on the number line.

10. $\frac{7}{8}$

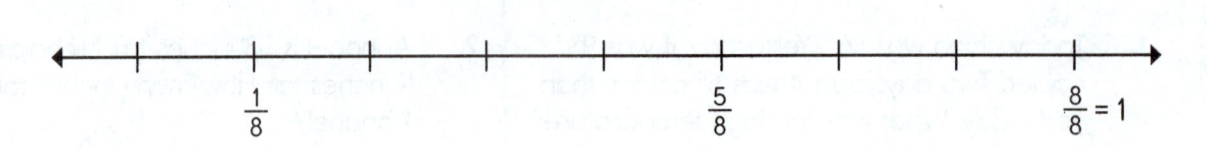

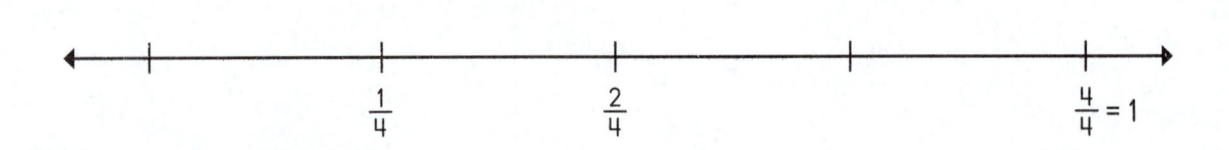

11. $\frac{3}{4}$

12. $\frac{12}{12}$

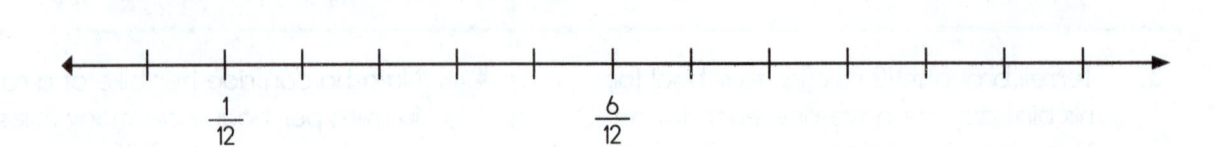

Complete each sentence with the future-tense form of the verb in parentheses.

13. Maria _____ for her science test tonight.
(study)

14. Angelo _____ his stepmother this weekend.
(visit)

15. Carrie _____ to the movies tomorrow.
(go)

16. Scott _____ his new book this evening.
(read)

17. Wendy _____ me her new bracelet when she returns.
(show)

Fast Fun Fact

Saturn is the only planet in our solar system that could float on water.

Suffixes/Parts of Speech

Skill IDs: CYD • K8V

DAY 16

Add a suffix to each word. Use -est, -tion, or -ty. Double, drop, or change some letters if needed. Then, write the meaning of the new word.

1. tasty _tastiest, most tasty_

2. act _____

3. safe _____

4. hungry _____

5. prepare _____

6. heavy _____

Circle the pronouns in each sentence.

7. I told her about Janelle's horse.

8. This piece of cake is for him.

9. Liz invited Garrett and me to the party.

10. The table is set for us.

11. We are too late to see the first show.

12. They will be happy to come along.

13. Snails and turtles have shells. They are protected by them.

43

DAY 16 — Language Arts
IXL Skill ID 62X

Complete each sentence with the correct word from the parentheses.

14. The baseball game went _____ for the Spartans right from the first inning. (well, better, best)

15. The first batter, Monroe, always hits _____. (well, better, best)

16. Monroe runs the bases _____ than most players on his team. (well, better, best)

17. Stanley, the second batter, usually hits even _____ than Monroe (well, better, best)

18. The pitcher threw his _____ pitches to Stanley. (well, better, best)

19. Stanley hit the ball _____, and it flew over the fence for a two-run home run. (well, better, best)

20. Things went _____ for the Tigers in the second half of the game than in the first. (badly, worse, worst)

21. The Tigers' best player seemed unfocused, and it got _____ as the game went on. (badly, worse, worst)

22. Maybe next week he will be able to concentrate _____. (well, better, best)

Mindful Moment

Look up the definition of the word *considerate*. Then, think of two ways that you can be considerate.

Reading Comprehension/Suffixes

DAY 17

Read the story. Then, write two details from the story in the order that they occurred.

Quinn and Phillip washed their dad's car. First, they filled a bucket with soapy water. Quinn got some old rags from the house while Phillip got the hose. They put soapy water all over the car and washed off the dirt. Next, they rinsed the car with water. To finish the job, Quinn and Phillip dried the car with some clean towels. They were both surprised when their dad gave them $5 each.

1. _____

2. _____

Each word below contains the suffix *-est*, *-tion*, or *-ty*. Circle each suffix. Then, write the base word.

3. safe(ty) safe

4. saddest _____

5. hungriest _____

6. preparation _____

7. invention _____

8. tasty _____

9. certainty _____

10. loyalty _____

11. direction _____

12. lovliest _____

Lucy Maud Montgomery

Lucy Maud Montgomery is famous for creating the character of Anne Shirley in the Anne of Green Gables series. Montgomery was born in 1874 on Prince Edward Island in Canada. She lived with her grandparents and went to class in a one-room schoolhouse. Her first poem was published when she was 17 years old. She wrote *Anne of Green Gables* in 1905, but it was not published until 1908. The book became a best-seller, and Montgomery wrote several other books based on the main character. Two films and at least seven TV shows have been made from the Anne of Green Gables series. Although Montgomery moved away from Prince Edward Island in 1911, all but one of her books are set there. Many people still visit the island today to see where Anne Shirley grew up.

13. What is the main idea of this passage?

   A. Lucy Maud Montgomery grew up on Prince Edward Island.

   B. Lucy Maud Montgomery is famous for writing *Anne of Green Gables*.

   C. Lucy Maud Montgomery was a schoolteacher.

14. Who is Anne Shirley? _____

15. What was Montgomery's early life like? _____
    _____

16. When was Montgomery's first poem published? _____

17. How can you tell that *Anne of Green Gables* was a popular book? _____
    _____

18. Why do many people visit Prince Edward Island today?
    _____

Multiplication/Parts of Speech

Day 18

Skill IDs: 9PM • Z6T

Multiply to find each product.

1. 16 × 5
2. 15 × 6
3. 28 × 3
4. 24 × 4

5. 47 × 2
6. 19 × 4
7. 38 × 2
8. 21 × 4

Write the past-tense form of each underlined verb.

9. A tadpole <u>hatches</u> from an egg in a pond. _____

10. It <u>looks</u> like a small fish at first. _____

11. The tadpole <u>uses</u> its tail to swim. _____

12. It <u>breathes</u> with gills. _____

13. Its appearance <u>changes</u> after a few weeks. _____

14. It <u>starts</u> to grow hind legs. _____

15. Its head <u>flattens</u>. _____

16. Its gills <u>vanish</u>. _____

17. Its tail <u>disappears</u>. _____

18. It <u>hops</u> onto dry land. _____

© Carson Dellosa Education

47

DAY 18

Skill IDs: M8H • GW2

Language Arts

Follow the directions using a dictionary.

19. Browse through the letter *H* words. Choose a word to write. _____

20. Write the meaning of the word you chose. _____
    _____

21. How many syllables does your word have? _____

22. What mark is used to show how words are divided into syllables? _____

Complete each sentence with the correct form of *good* or *bad* from the parentheses.

23. The weatherperson said that we will have _____ weather on Thursday. (good, better, best)

24. She said that the weather this weekend will be _____ than today. (good, better, best)

25. Sunday will have the _____ weather this week. (good, better, best)

26. Parts of the country are having _____ storms. (bad, worse, worst)

27. The weatherperson is predicting that the _____ of the snow is coming soon. (bad, worse, worst)

28. Florida usually has _____ weather in the winter. (good, better, best)

Let's Play Today *See page 12.

Do 10 shoulder shrugs.

Reading Comprehension

Elisha Otis

Have you ever ridden in an elevator? Elevators make it much easier for people to get from one floor to another in a tall building. At one time, elevators were not as safe as they are today. Elisha Otis helped change that. Early elevators used ropes that sometimes broke, sending the people riding the elevator to the ground. To make elevators safer, Otis made wooden guide rails to go on each side of an elevator. Cables ran through the rails and were connected to a spring that would pull the elevator up if the cables broke. Otis displayed his invention for the first time at the New York Crystal Palace Exhibition in 1853. His safety elevators were used in buildings as tall as the Eiffel Tower in Paris, France, and the Empire State Building in New York City, New York. Otis died in 1861. His sons, Charles and Norton, continued to sell his design, and many elevators today still have the Otis name on them.

1. What is the main idea of this passage?

    A. The Otis family still sells elevators today.

    B. At one time, elevators were unsafe to use.

    C. Elisha Otis found a way to make elevators safe.

2. Why were early elevators dangerous? _____

_____

3. What did the spring in Otis's elevators do? _____

_____

4. What are two buildings that used Otis's elevator design? _____

_____

5. What did Otis's sons do after his death? _____

_____

DAY 19

IXL Skill IDs **PNV • XS8** — Search for these skill IDs on IXL.com for more practice!

Multiplication/Language Arts

Time yourself as you solve the problems. Can you answer them correctly in one minute?

6. 9 × 7 = _____

7. 4 × 6 = _____

8. 8 × 5 = _____

9. 2 × 9 = _____

10. 5 × 3 = _____

11. 8 × 8 = _____

12. 6 × 9 = _____

13. 3 × 7 = _____

14. 5 × 4 = _____

15. 7 × 7 = _____

16. 6 × 8 = _____

17. 4 × 4 = _____

Fill in the blanks to complete the friendly letter. Use correct capitalization.

_____ (date)

_____ , (greeting)

I'm having a _____ summer. So far, the best part of the summer has been

_____

_____

_____

_____ , (closing)

_____ (your name)

Addition/Parts of Speech

Add to find each sum.

1. 78
   81
   + 65

2. 51
   21
   + 83

3. 81
   57
   + 52

4. 34
   67
   + 24

5. 76
   53
   + 19

6. 49
   74
   + 84

7. 76
   34
   + 51

8. 28
   54
   + 84

Read each verb. Write A if it is a present-tense action verb. Write L if it is a linking verb.

9. __A__ bloom

10. __L__ is

11. _____ has

12. _____ hatch

13. _____ have

14. _____ seem

15. _____ pretend

16. _____ stir

17. _____ becomes

18. _____ study

19. _____ walk

20. _____ hold

21. _____ were

22. _____ am

23. _____ skip

24. _____ was

DAY 20

Skill IDs: 7LG • RQ5

Division/Parts of Speech

Divide to find each quotient.

25. 2)84   26. 2)62   27. 2)68   28. 3)93

29. 7)70   30. 5)55   31. 3)69   32. 9)99

Read each set of sentences. Write *P* next to sentences in the past tense, *PR* next to sentences in the present tense, and *F* next to sentences in the future tense.

33. A. Mischa ran to the market. _____
     B. Mischa will run around the block. _____
     C. Mischa runs to the park with Lea. _____

34. A. I am having green beans with dinner. _____
     B. I will have a salad tomorrow. _____
     C. I had broccoli yesterday. _____

35. A. Troy will catch the ball. _____
     B. Troy catches the ball. _____
     C. Troy caught the ball. _____

36. A. He will go to the new school. _____
     B. He went to the new school. _____
     C. He goes to the new school. _____

Fast Fun Fact

The first food grown in space and eaten was red romaine lettuce.

Science Experiment — BONUS

Coffee Filter Chromatography

Chromatography is a process used to separate colors. This activity shows how part of the ink in water-soluble markers can be dissolved. Other, more soluble colors will travel up a coffee filter with water.

Materials:

- 3 water-soluble markers (not permanent markers)
- 3 drinking glasses
- ruler
- coffee filter
- masking tape
- water
- scissors

Procedure:

Pour water into each glass so that it is about a half-inch (1.3 centimeters) deep. Label each glass and marker *1, 2,* or *3* using masking tape and the markers. Cut the coffee filter into three strips, one for each marker. Use the water-soluble markers to make one large dot one-third of the way up each coffee filter strip. Do this for all three markers. Place each coffee filter strip in the glass with the same number as the marker. The ink dots should be near, but not under, the water. Let the strips absorb the water.

1. What effect does the water have on the ink dots? _____

    _____

2. What happened differently to each of the three different ink dots? _____

    _____

    _____

3. Which marker's ink traveled the highest on a coffee filter strip? List the other markers in order from highest to lowest.

    _____

    _____

4. What does *water-soluble* mean? _____

BONUS Skill ID **Z7A** — Search for this skill ID on IXL.com for more practice!

Science Experiment

Speed Racer

How is the height of a ramp related to the speed of a toy?

Kinetic energy is the energy of motion. Potential energy is stored energy, or the energy of position.

Materials:

- ruler
- toy car
- stopwatch
- wooden ramp of any size

Procedure:

Raise one end of the ramp to the lowest height (about 1.5 inches [4 centimeters]) required for the toy car to roll from one end to the other. Place the car at the top of the ramp, and use the stopwatch to time it as it rolls to the bottom of the ramp. Record the speed of the car and the height of the ramp on the chart below. Repeat the activity two more times, raising the height of the ramp each time.

Trial	Height	Time
1		
2		
3		

1. What is the relationship between the height of the ramp and the speed of the object?

   _____

2. What surfaces might cause the toy car to roll faster or slower? _____

   _____

3. Try another object, such as a golf or tennis ball. What happens to the speed of the object if it has more mass? _____

4. What is the purpose of the question in bold below the title of the experiment?

   _____

5. How is the graph helpful in organizing the data? _____

   _____

Social Studies Activity

IXL Skill ID **5GB** BONUS

Prime Lines

Lines of longitude are imaginary lines that run north to south on a map. They are marked in degrees (°) and help us find locations around the world. The prime meridian is the line at 0° longitude. The lines of longitude on a map are measured in 15° segments from the prime meridian. Places east of the prime meridian have the letter *E* after their degrees. Places west of the prime meridian have the letter *W* after their degrees.

Study the map. Then, answer the questions.

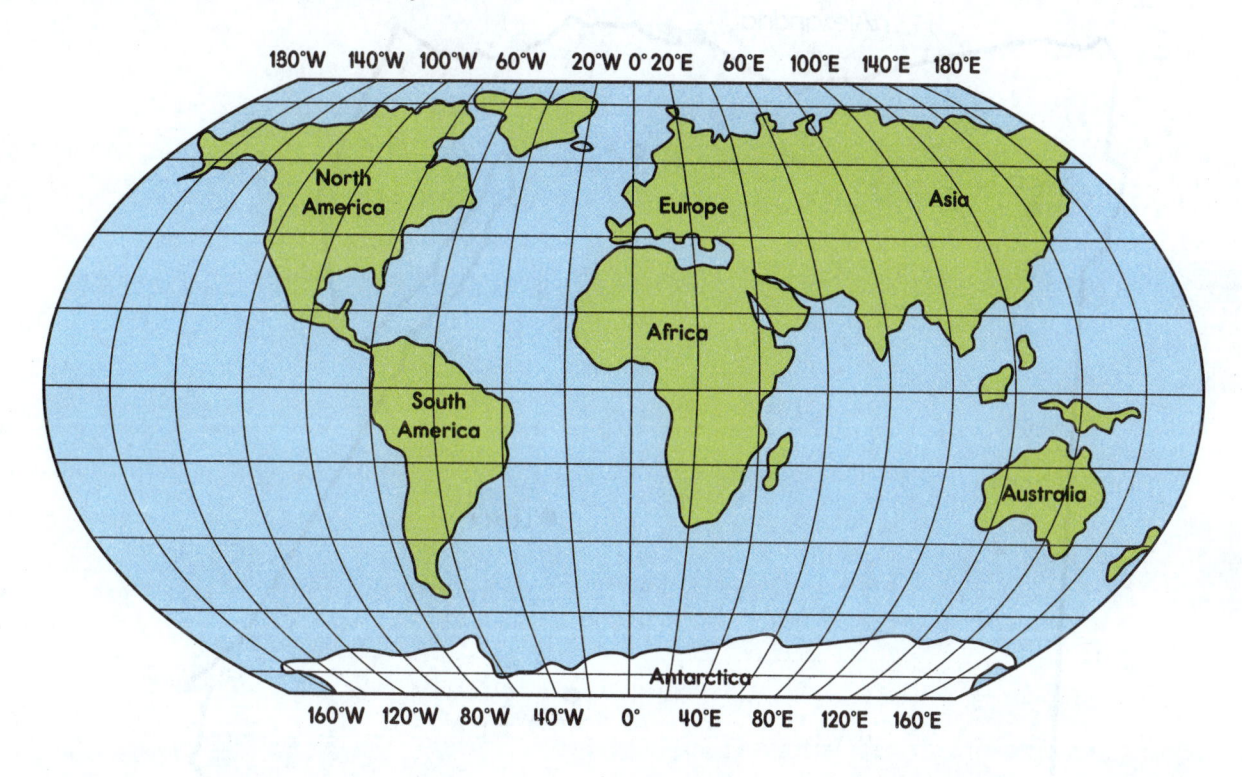

1. The prime meridian is at _____° longitude.

2. For locations in South America, the longitude should be followed by the letter _____.

3. For locations in most of Africa, the longitude should be followed by the letter _____.

4. Use an orange crayon or marker to trace the prime meridian.

© Carson Dellosa Education

55

BONUS

Social Studies Activity

Map Scale

A map scale represents distance on a map. A map cannot be shown at actual size, so it must be made smaller to fit on paper. On the map below, 1 cm = 100 km.

Study the map of Egypt. Measure the distance between dots with a ruler. Then, change the centimeters to kilometers to find the actual distance between each pair of cities.

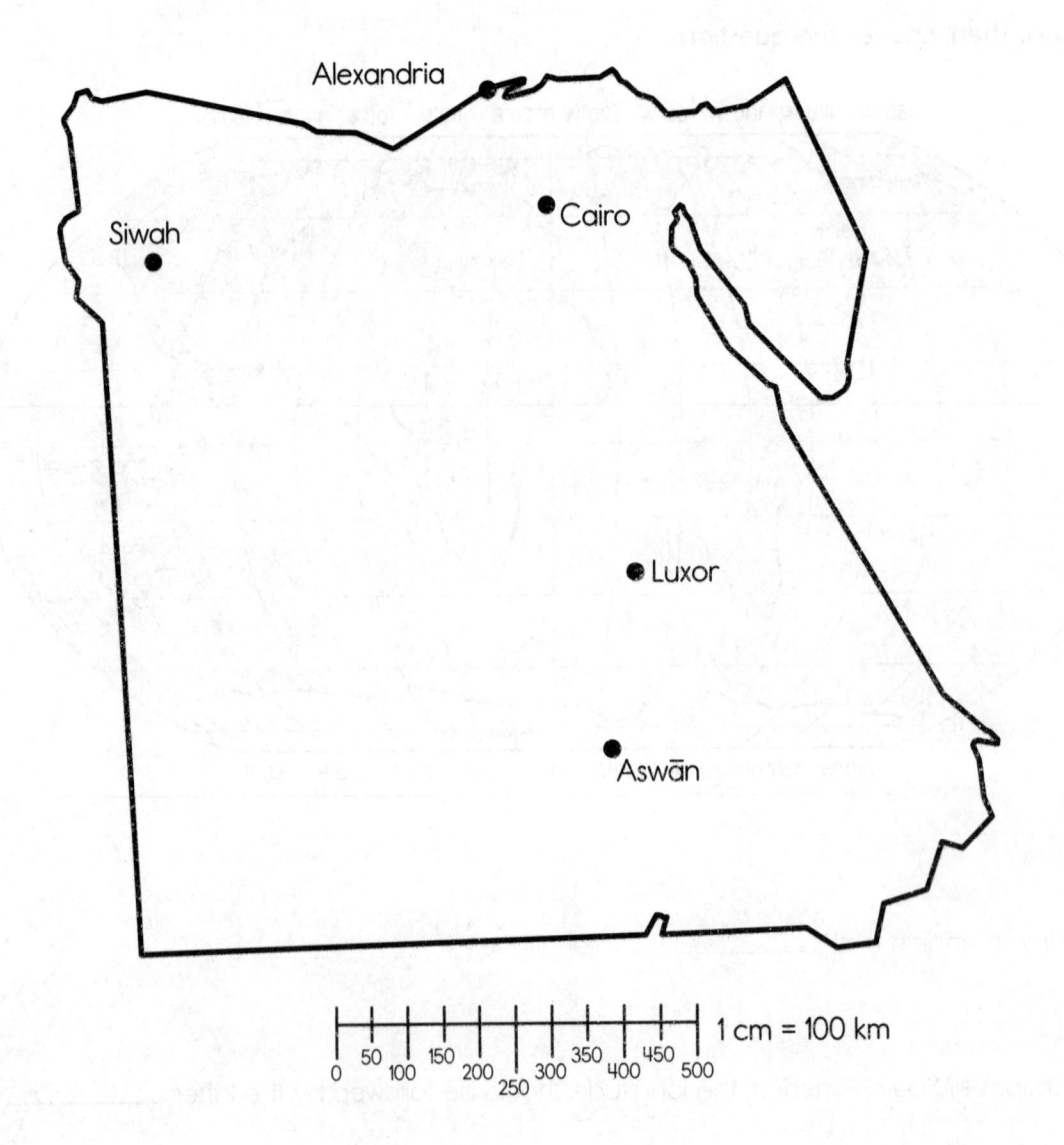

[Map of Egypt showing Alexandria, Siwah, Cairo, Luxor, and Aswān, with a scale bar marked 0, 50, 100, 150, 200, 250, 300, 350, 400, 450, 500; 1 cm = 100 km]

1. Cairo to Luxor _____
2. Cairo to Alexandria _____
3. Cairo to Siwah _____
4. Siwah to Aswān _____

© Carson Dellosa Education

Social Studies Activity

Using a Map

Write the letter of the physical feature next to its name. Use an atlas if you need help.

1. _____ Rocky Mountains
2. _____ Great Lakes
3. _____ Rio Grande
4. _____ Atlantic Ocean
5. _____ Great Salt Lake
6. _____ Great Basin
7. _____ Mississippi River
8. _____ Appalachian Mountains
9. _____ Sierra Nevada Mountains
10. _____ Pacific Ocean

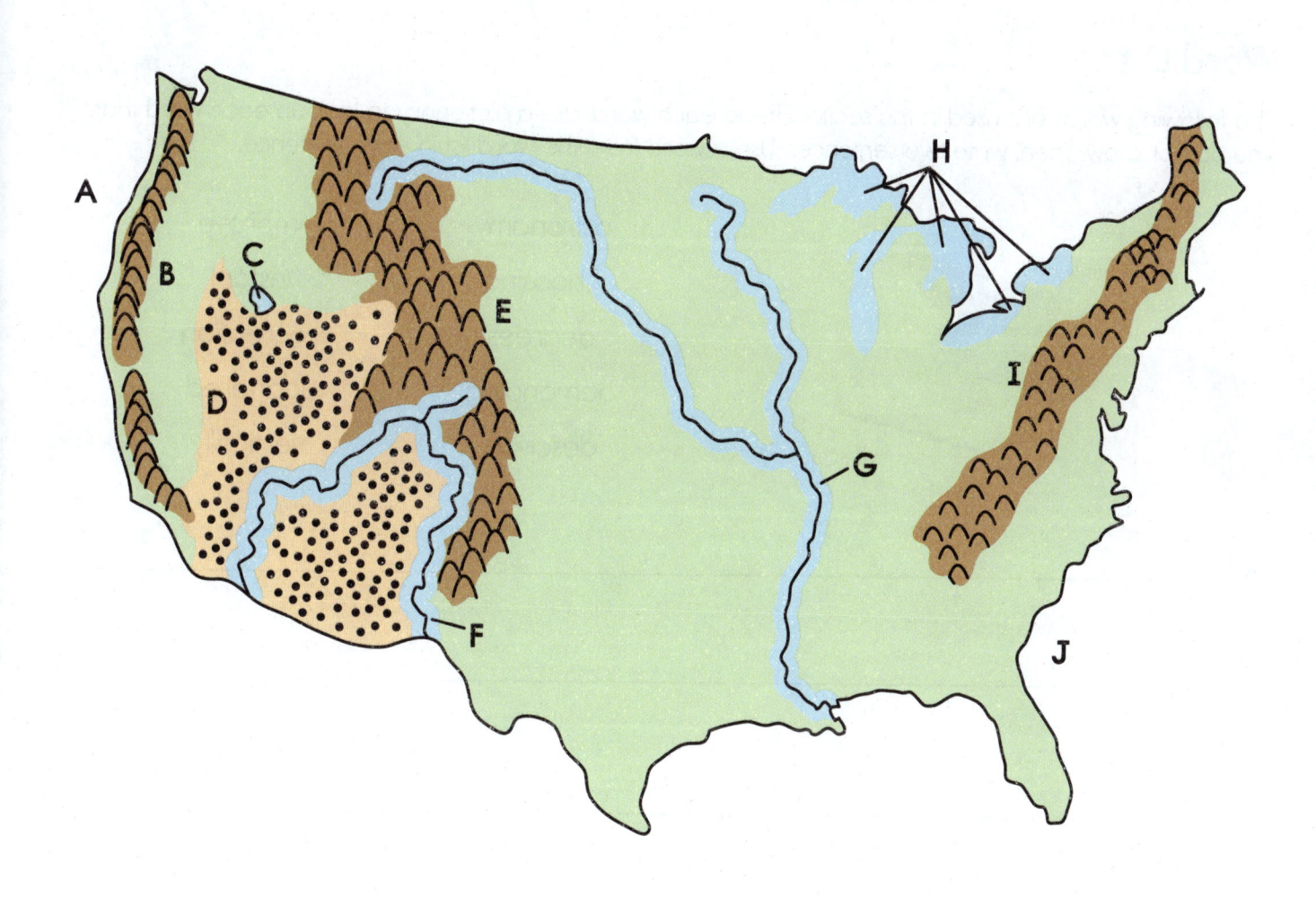

SECTION 2

Monthly Goals

Think of three goals to set for yourself this month. For example, you may want to exercise for 20 minutes each day. Write your goals on the lines and review them with an adult.

Place a sticker next to each of your goals that you complete. Feel proud that you have met your goals!

1. _____ PLACE STICKER

2. _____ PLACE STICKER

3. _____ PLACE STICKER

Word List

The following words are used in this section. Read each word. Use a dictionary to look up each word that you do not know. Then, write two sentences. Use a word from the word list in each sentence.

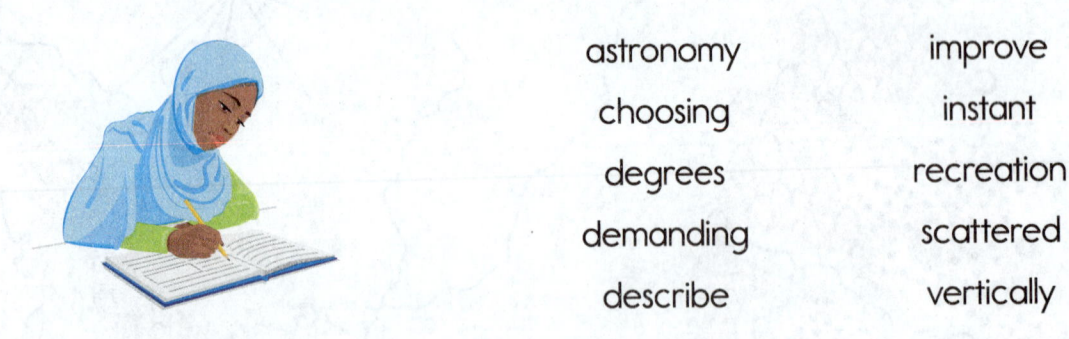

astronomy	improve
choosing	instant
degrees	recreation
demanding	scattered
describe	vertically

4. _____

_____

5. _____

_____

Introduction to Strength

This section includes Let's Play Today and Mindful Moments activities that focus on strength. These activities are designed to help you spend less time on a screen and more time developing healthy emotional and physical habits. If you have limited mobility, feel free to modify any suggested activity or choose a different one from the list on the following page.

Let's Play Today

Like flexibility, strength is necessary to be healthy. You might think being strong means lifting an enormous amount of weight. But strength is much more than just the ability to pick up heavy barbells. Strength is built by being physically active on a daily basis. As a toddler, you walked down the sidewalk. Now you can run across a baseball field. Look how strong you've become!

Everyday activities, fun exercises, and enjoyable games help you gain strength. Take a walk, do a classic exercise such as push-ups, or play a game of basketball or tag to build your physical strength.

Set realistic, achievable goals to improve your physical strength based on your ability and the activities you enjoy. Over the summer months, keep track of these goals and celebrate when you achieve them. Then set new ones!

Mindful Moments

Having strength of character on the inside is just as important as having physical strength on the outside. Being a strong person on the inside can be shown by being honest, facing a fear, helping others, standing up for someone who needs a friend, or choosing to do the right thing when presented with a difficult situation. Think about times when you have had inner strength that has helped you handle a situation. Be proud of the moments you have shown inner strength. This positive inner growth on the inside is as important as physical growth on the outside.

Engaging Online Practice

Bring learning to life with fun, interactive activities on IXL! Look for the Skill ID box and type the 3-digit code into the search bar on IXL.com or the IXL mobile app. Ten questions per day are free!

IXL Skill IDs: 5UN • D9K

SECTION 2

Let's Play Today

Get up and moving with these Let's Play Today activities. Section 2 focuses on strength. Strengthening exercises make your bones and muscles stronger. Strong bones and muscles help prevent injury and speed up recovery from injury. Use this list in addition to or as a replacement for any Let's Play Today suggestions on the activity pages. This list was developed to be inclusive of a variety of abilities. Choose the ones that are a good fit for you! Make modifications as needed. These activities may require adult supervision. See page 2 for full caution information.

Lava Pit:

Hop from pillow to pillow on an imaginary bed of lava. Start with just 3-4 pillows and repeat it two times. Over time, gradually add pillows to work up to a longer, more complex path of pillows. Repeat hopping on the longer path 10 times.

Frog Hops:

Crouch down with your hands on the floor in a frog-like position. Hop forward like a frog 3-4 times. Over time, gradually increase the number of hops until you get to 15.

Shadow Fun:

Go outside on a sunny day and make sure you can see your shadow. If you are by yourself, practice shadow boxing. Bend your arms at the elbows and bring your hands back to your body. Make a fist with each hand. Extend one arm at a time to mimic a boxing motion. If someone is outside with you, trace each other's shadow with chalk. Hold a pose that works your muscles, such as standing on one leg or flexing your arms.

Balloon Back-and-Forth:

Either seated or standing, hit a balloon up into the air to another person. That person will hit it back to you. Keep track of how many times you can hit it to each other without it touching the ground. Try to increase your score.

Swim Like a Fish:

Wearing a life jacket in the shallow end of a pool, try swimming like a fish! Use flippers to help. See how many different ways to swim you can come up with. For example, swim like you have a fish tail, swim without using your arms, swim with flippers on your hands, or roll around.

60 © Carson Dellosa Education

Multiplication & Division/Language Arts

Skill ID: 67L

DAY 1

Draw a line to match each related division and multiplication problem.

1. 65 ÷ 5   A. 6 × 4
2. 24 ÷ 6   B. 17 × 3
3. 64 ÷ 8   C. 8 × 8
4. 51 ÷ 3   D. 13 × 5

5. 72 ÷ 4   A. 18 × 4
6. 50 ÷ 2   B. 43 × 2
7. 56 ÷ 4   C. 25 × 2
8. 86 ÷ 2   D. 14 × 4

Write a book report about your favorite book. Use the outline to help you.

Title _____

Author _____

Main characters _____

Where and when does the story take place? _____

What is the main theme of the book? _____

_____

Why did you like the book? _____

_____

Punctuation/Writing

Quotation marks set off what someone says. Write quotation marks in each sentence around what each person says.

9. Uncle Emillio said, "I will pack a picnic lunch."

10. Where is the big beach ball? asked Malik.

11. Mei exclaimed, That is a wonderful idea!

12. Come and do your work, Grandma said, or you can't go with us.

13. Yesterday, said Ella, I saw a pretty robin in the tree by my window.

14. I will always take care of my pets, promised Theodore.

15. Rachel said, Maybe we should have practiced more.

16. Dr. Jacobs asked, How are you, Kade?

On a separate sheet of paper, write a story about a real or imaginary place you would like to visit this summer.

Consider the following questions before you begin to write.

- Who are the characters in the story?
- Where does the story take place?
- How does the story begin?
- What happens next?
- How does the story end?

Mindful Moment

Why is it important to be someone people can trust? Write your answer on a separate sheet of paper.

Writing/Parts of Speech

Do you think that students should have to wear school uniforms? Why or why not? State your opinion and provide reasons that support it.

_____
_____
_____
_____
_____
_____
_____
_____
_____

Common nouns are general names for people, places, or things. Proper nouns name specific people, places, or things and begin with uppercase letters. Write each noun under the correct heading.

	Common Nouns	Proper Nouns
Monday		
ocean	_____	_____
class		
November	_____	_____
holiday		
July	_____	_____
boat		
beans	_____	_____
Rex		
North Carolina	_____	_____

DAY 2

Skill IDs: GHA • VNC

Reading Comprehension/Vocabulary

Read the passage. Then, answer the questions.

Choosing a Pet

Before you decide what kind of pet you would like to own, there are some things you should think about. First, find out how much care the pet will need. Dogs need to be walked; horses need to be exercised; cats need a place to scratch. All pets need to be kept clean and well fed. You should also think about where your pet would live. Big pets need a lot of room, while little pets do not need as much room.

1. What is the topic of the passage?
   - A. caring for a dog
   - B. choosing a pet
   - C. feeding big pets
   - D. where pets live

2. What is the main idea?
   - A. finding good homes for pets
   - B. things to do when choosing a pet
   - C. things to think about before choosing a pet
   - D. bring your pet home

Write the correct homophone from the word bank to complete each sentence.

| too | two | to | cent | scent | sent |

3. The _____ kittens played with the ball.

4. A penny equals one _____.

5. My aunt asked me to go _____ the store.

6. Malcolm _____ a letter to his friend.

7. I will clean my desk and the table _____.

8. The flower has a sweet _____.

Prefixes/Parts of Speech

Skill IDs: QR5 • ESB

DAY 3

Write the prefix *re-* or *un-* in each blank to complete each sentence. On the line, write the meaning of the new word.

1. Please _____ move your shoes before you come in. _____

2. That was an _____ usual movie. _____

3. I would like to _____ new the streaming service subscription. _____

4. That was an _____ common rainstorm. _____

5. You will have to _____ tell the story later. _____

A pronoun is a word that takes the place of a noun. Read each sentence. Then, circle the noun(s) that each underlined pronoun is replacing.

6. Imani has a (computer). She keeps <u>it</u> on her desk.

7. Marta forgot her umbrella. She went home to get <u>it</u>.

8. Benji asked Juan if <u>he</u> would teach him to hit a baseball.

9. Amira and Becca both collect seashells. Sometimes, <u>they</u> trade with each other.

10. Nia plays the violin, and sometimes <u>she</u> sings, too.

11. We gave our dog a new toy. Fido barked when he saw <u>it</u>.

12. Our school bus is always crowded, and <u>it</u> is usually noisy, too.

© Carson Dellosa Education

65

DAY 3

IXL Skill IDs: NLS • XKD

Search for these skill IDs on IXL.com for more practice!

Spelling

Read each group of words. Circle each correctly spelled word and write it on the line.

13. warm   wirm   warme   _____

14. wurried   woried   worried   _____

15. woh   hwo   who   _____

16. weigh   weh   wiegh   _____

17. wint   wat   want   _____

Read each sentence. Cross out the word that is spelled incorrectly. Rewrite the word with the correct spelling.

18. The dinner tasted wondirful.   _____

19. How many childrin are on the playground?   _____

20. Do you know wair my hat is?   _____

21. I lost my two front teath.   _____

Let's Play Today *See page 60

Learn to do a demanding up-down. Begin by running in place. Then, drop to the ground with your chest to the floor and your legs straight behind you. Do one push-up. Then, jump back to your feet and run in place again.

Geometry/Writing

Name each figure by its points and label it with the correct symbol.

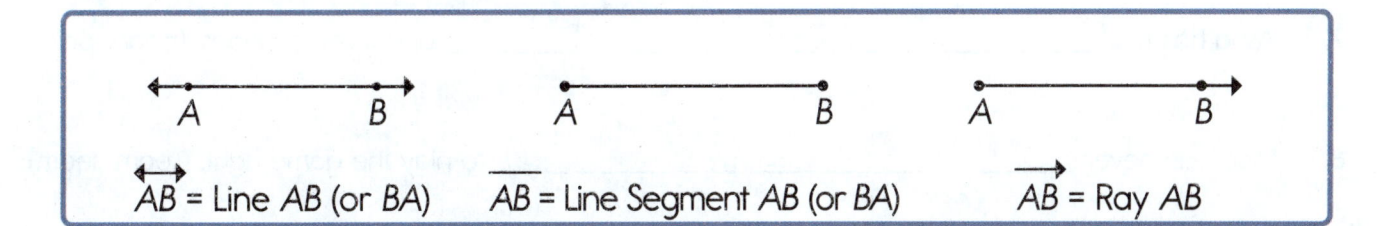

$\overleftrightarrow{AB}$ = Line AB (or BA) $\overline{AB}$ = Line Segment AB (or BA) $\overrightarrow{AB}$ = Ray AB

1. $\overrightarrow{AB}$ = Ray AB

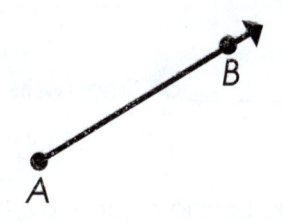

2. $\overleftrightarrow{GH}$ = Line GH (or HG)

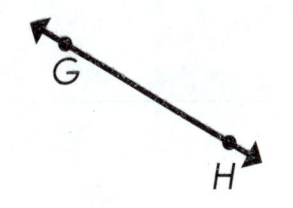

3. $\overline{LM}$ = Line Segment LM (or ML)

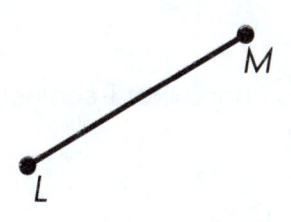

4. $\overleftrightarrow{CD}$ = Line CD (or DC)

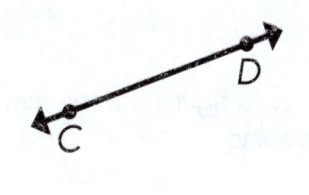

5. $\overrightarrow{UT}$ = Ray UT

6. $\overrightarrow{WX}$ = Ray WX

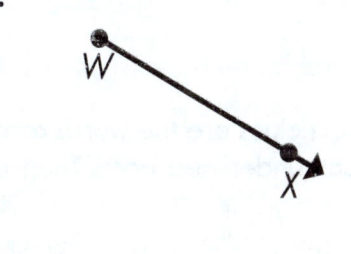

What would you do if you woke up and found out you could be invisible?

DAY 4

Vocabulary

Write the correct homophone from the parentheses to complete each sentence.

7. Asha has two _____ and three oranges. (pears, pairs)

8. Nico can never _____ to play the game right. (seam, seem)

9. Dad will sift the _____ for the cookies. (flour, flower)

10. I hope that I can get everything _____ on time. (write, right)

11. Quan _____ the baking contest. (won, one)

12. The bread _____ was very sticky. (doe, dough)

Context clues are the words around a word you do not know. Use context clues to figure out the meaning of each underlined word. Then, circle the letter next to the word's correct meaning.

13. My brother and I often <u>argue</u> about who gets to use the computer.

    A. work   **B.** disagree   **C.** study

14. The <u>official</u> told us not to enter the building until 8 o'clock.

    A. person in charge   **B.** nurse   **C.** child

15. Josie saw an <u>unusual</u> light in the sky and asked her father what it was.

    A. dark   **B.** star   **C.** different

16. The <u>cardinal</u> in my backyard is a beautiful sight. I love his bright red color and sweet song.

    A. singer   **B.** branch   **C.** bird with red feathers

17. Mom asked me to turn down the <u>volume</u> on the TV because it was too loud.

    A. noise level   **B.** book   **C.** color

Measurement/Geometry

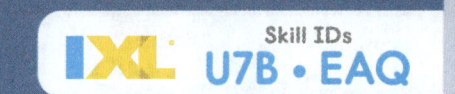

Use the clock to answer each question.

1. What time does the clock show?

   _____

2. How long will it take for the minute hand to move from 6 to 5?

   _____

Write the number of sides and vertices for each polygon.

3. _____ sides _____ vertices

4. _____ sides _____ vertices

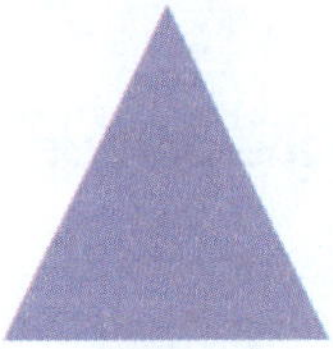

5. _____ sides _____ vertices

6. _____ sides _____ vertices

7. _____ sides _____ vertices

8. _____ sides _____ vertices

9. Which three shapes have the same number of sides and vertices?

   _____ _____ _____

DAY 5

Addition/Parts of Speech

Add to find each sum.

10.   4,340
      5,433
    + 3,238

11.   356
        674
      + 380

12.   54
        39
      + 73

13.   634
       198
     + 518

14.   47
        34
      + 99

15.   321
       436
     + 548

16.   9,418
      8,009
    + 7,245

17.   4,259
      1,564
    + 2,873

An adverb is a word that modifies a verb. Circle the adverb in each sentence. Then, underline the verb that the adverb modifies.

18. On Independence Day, we (usually) go to the parade.

19. We drive slowly because of traffic.

20. The parade often begins with a marching band.

21. The huge crowd cheers excitedly.

22. My favorite part is when the big floats pass near us.

23. All of the floats are decorated beautifully.

Fast Fun Fact

Fireworks have been used since at least 200 BCE in China, but not for celebrating. Instead they were used to scare off enemies!

Multiplication/Vocabulary

DAY 6

Complete each multiplication chart.

1.

× 2	
4	
8	
3	6
6	
9	
5	10
7	

2.

× 3	
3	9
7	
5	
2	
6	18
4	
8	

3.

× 4	
10	
5	20
8	
4	
7	
6	
9	

4.

× 5	
9	
2	
6	
3	15
5	
7	
4	

Write the correct word from the word bank to complete each sentence.

Word Bank:
cottage
quarter
curtains
circus
bell
pictures
pennies
market

5. Look at all of the funny _____ in this book.

6. You can buy bread and milk at the _____.

7. We live in a small _____.

8. This pencil costs a _____.

9. I am saving a lot of _____ in a jar.

10. The clowns at the _____ were great.

11. When you hear the _____, run fast.

12. We have white _____ on our windows.

71

DAY 6

Division/Parts of Speech

Skill IDs
2K3 • 8YP

Divide to find each quotient.

13. 6)360   14. 8)480   15. 4)440   16. 7)630

17. 8)560   18. 7)350   19. 9)720   20. 7)210

Write the correct past-tense form of the irregular verb in parentheses to complete each sentence.

21. Our teacher _____ our class a book about insects. (read)

22. I _____ Mr. Lee before he was my teacher. (know)

23. Ms. Kemp _____ us that we could eat outside today. (tell)

24. Raul _____ that I can borrow his jump rope anytime. (say)

25. I _____ a bird chirping in a tree. (hear)

26. Cody _____ a new baseball glove today. (buy)

27. Sho and Gene each _____ an apple for a snack. (eat)

28. Jaime and her dad _____ a ramp for her wheelchair. (build)

Mindful Moment

Think back to a time you made a mistake. What is one good thing that came from it? Maybe you learned something or showed courage in making the mistake.

Addition/Parts of Speech

Skill IDs: P5U • 29B

DAY 7

Draw a straight line through three numbers that, when added together, total each sum provided.

1. Sum: 78

20	28	14
16	32	42
19	18	13

2. Sum: 110

16	33	64
39	22	44
51	10	72

3. Sum: 251

71	47	18
82	20	46
98	43	33

4. Sum: 149

15	93	24
63	25	33
63	25	61

5. Sum: 506

94	100	90
88	206	58
79	200	96

6. Sum: 189

94	100	90
88	20	58
79	10	96

Write the correct past- or present-tense form of the verb in parentheses to complete each sentence.

7. My friends and I like to _____ clay animals. (make)

8. Yesterday, we _____ the clay into different shapes. (roll)

9. Jeremy _____ making a clay hippo yesterday. (enjoy)

10. Our teacher _____ us bake the clay animals. (help)

11. After they were baked and cooled, we _____ them. (paint)

DAY 7

Skill IDs: ZQG • SGP

Sentence Structure/Measurement

Read each group of words. Write the words in the correct order to make complete sentences. Use correct punctuation and capitalization.

12. rode hill the I down on bike a _____

_____

13. garden a our mom backyard I planted and in my _____

_____

14. themselves elephants animals when braced all the sneezed the of _____

_____

Find the area of each shape.

15.

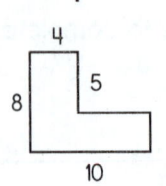

area = _____ square units

16.

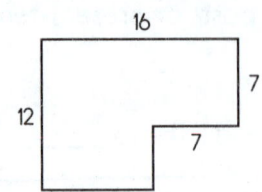

area = _____ square units

17.

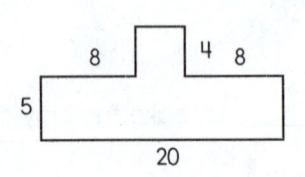

area = _____ square units

18.

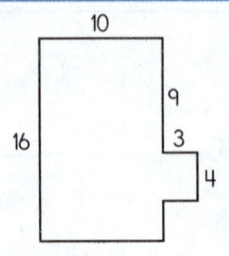

area = _____ square units

74 © Carson Dellosa Education

Punctuation/Measurement

Add commas where they belong in each phrase or sentence.

1. My family visits Spring Grove Minnesota every year in the summer.

2. Dear Grandpa

3. Yours truly

4. On October 9 2024 Carolyn saw the play.

5. My aunt and uncle live in North Branch New York.

6. Dear Jon

7. January 1 2025

8. Paris Texas is located in the northeastern part of the state.

Circle the measurement from the parentheses that correctly completes each sentence.

9. A bathtub could hold up to (150 milliliters, 150 liters) of water.

10. A flower vase could hold up to (1 liter, 1 milliliter) of water.

11. A bike would weigh (10 grams, 10 kilograms).

12. An orange would weigh (100 grams, 100 ounces).

13. An ear of corn would be (11 inches, 11 yards) long.

14. A pencil would be (15 meters, 15 centimeters) long.

DAY 8

Division

Divide to find each quotient.

15. 2)184   16. 7)210   17. 7)231   18. 5)625

19. 9)459   20. 4)256   21. 9)144   22. 5)355

23. 9)162   24. 8)320   25. 6)132   26. 8)136

Solve the problem.

27. There are 270 third-grade students going on a field trip. They will fit equally on 3 buses. How many students will be on each bus? _____ students

Let's Play Today *See page 60.

Create a fitness obstacle course. Mark four different spots to run to. At each spot, complete a different fitness challenge, such as 10 push-ups.

Division/Spelling

Answer each question.

1. How many 6s are in 18? _____
2. How many 9s are in 18? _____
3. How many 4s are in 20? _____
4. How many 8s are in 32? _____

Read each sentence. If the underlined word is spelled correctly, write *correct*. If it is spelled incorrectly, rewrite the word with the correct spelling.

5. I'd like a glass of water. _____

6. Do you know where they've been today? _____

7. Be carefull with that knife. _____

8. My mom was very unhappy today. _____

9. What did Joni plant in her gardin? _____

10. We looked at all of the babyies in the hospital. _____

11. Aunt Mary canned 10 pounds of cherries. _____

12. He waved at us from the window. _____

13. Did you like the new movee? _____

14. Remember to set your alarm clock. _____

Reading Comprehension

Read the story. Then, answer the questions.

Good Friends

    Robert and Kaye are two of my best friends. We have gone to school together since we were in kindergarten. We even go to summer camp and the recreation center together. There are many reasons why I like to spend time with them. Robert always lets me borrow his skateboard. He knows that if I had a skateboard, I would let him borrow it. Robert is a person I can count on, too. When we are out riding our bikes together, Kaye sometimes lets me ride in front while she rides behind me. She understands that one way to be a good friend is by taking turns and being fair.

15. How is Robert a good friend? _____

_____

16. Is Kaye a fair person? Why? _____

_____

17. List three things that the friends do together. _____

_____

18. What does it mean to say you can "count on" someone? _____

_____

Problem Solving/Vocabulary

Skill IDs: SRL • 95E — DAY 10

Solve each word problem. Show your work.

1. There are 48 people coming to a family reunion. One-fourth of them live out of state. How many live in-state?

2. At the reunion, 3 meals will be served. Each person will use one plate for each meal. How many plates are needed?

3. The oldest person coming to the reunion is 84. The youngest person is 3. How many times older is the oldest person than the youngest person?

4. Of the people coming to the reunion, 16 are children. Each child will get 8 water balloons. How many water balloons are needed?

Read each pair of words. For each pair, write one way the two things are alike and one way they are different.

5. cabin, tent _____

6. whistle, sing _____

DAY 10

Skill IDs: EHT • Y7G
Search for these skill IDs on IXL.com for more practice!

Subtraction/Parts of Speech

Subtract to find each difference.

7. 943
   −549

8. 7,452
   −6,789

9. 526
   −498

10. 754
   −528

11. 751
   −439

12. 8,236
   −5,548

13. 7,840
   −4,251

14. 6,324
   −3,489

In the sentences below, circle the helping verbs. Underline the main verbs.

15. The girls were planning a sleepover for Friday.

16. Samir has read that book at least three times.

17. Colin has used that same duffel bag for the last five years.

18. Brandy will bring snacks to the game.

19. Zara is getting a dog tomorrow.

20. Tonight, we are studying for the quiz at Annie's house.

Fast Fun Fact

Humans have kept dogs as pets for about 10,000 years.

Addition/Language Arts

Add to find each sum.

1.
```
  6,898
  5,433
+ 2,154
```

2.
```
  8,459
  4,908
+ 4,356
```

3.
```
   525
   653
+  896
```

4.
```
  2,147
  3,255
+ 2,256
```

5.
```
   654
   452
+  138
```

6.
```
  7,092
  5,405
+ 6,124
```

7.
```
  5,768
  6,937
+ 7,034
```

8.
```
  4,265
  5,124
+ 6,489
```

A metaphor is a figure of speech in which two things are compared without using the words *like* or *as*. Read each metaphor. Write the names of the two things that are being compared.

9. The falling snowflakes were tiny dancers whirling through the sky.

    _____ and _____

10. The highway was a parking lot, and it took us hours to get home.

    _____ and _____

11. The tornado was a powerful train heading straight for the tiny town.

    _____ and _____

12. Dara's fingers were icicles after two hours of sledding.

    _____ and _____

DAY 11

Place Value/Vocabulary

Write a number for each expanded form.

13.	14.	15.	16.
7,000 + 500 + 60 + 2	1,000 + 800 + 40 + 7	4,000 + 200 + 80	9,000 + 900 + 90 + 9
7,562	_____	_____	_____

Use the words from the word bank to solve the crossword puzzle.

Across

17. very sure
18. to make something look larger
19. to go behind
20. needs to be done now
21. to care for the sick

Down

22. to spin
23. to send back
24. not better

Word bank: urgent, positive, nurse, worse, return, magnify, follow, twirl

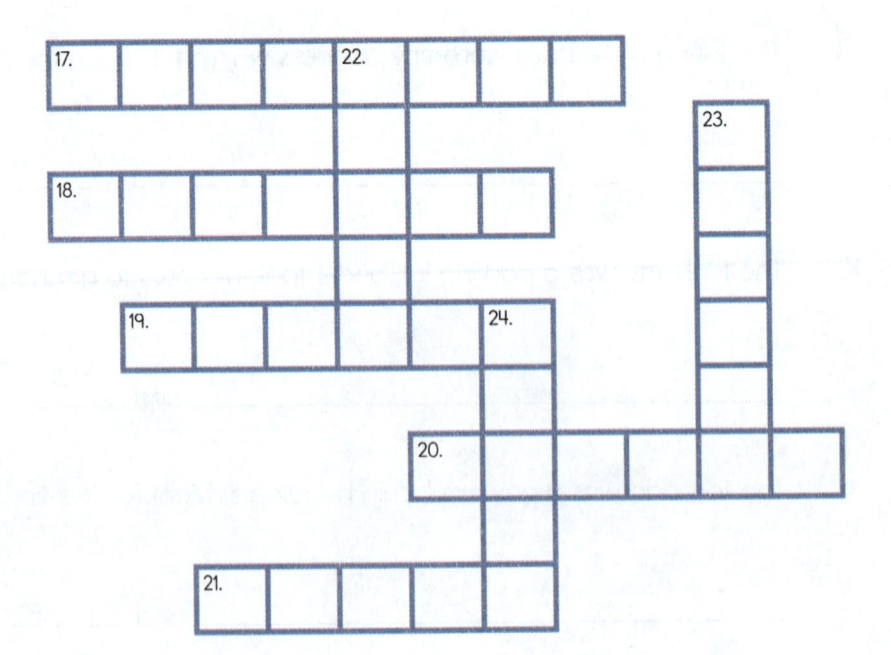

Mindful Moment

On a separate sheet of paper, write "I am" on five lines. Finish the sentences with positive facts about yourself.

Place Value/Geometry

Write each number. Then, write its expanded form.

1. five hundred sixty-one _____

2. four thousand eight hundred twenty-six _____

Count how many are in each set. Write each number.

3. _____

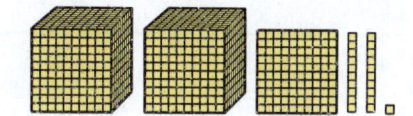

4. _____

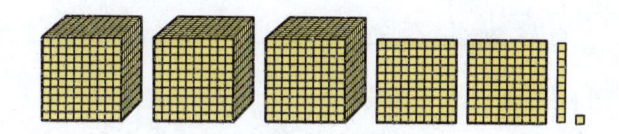

Write the letter of each definition next to the correct geometry term.

5. _____ parallel lines

6. _____ perpendicular lines

7. _____ vertex

8. _____ face

9. _____ edge

10. _____ ray

11. _____ line segment

12. _____ angle

A. line with one endpoint that continues in one direction

B. the endpoint of three line segments on a solid figure

C. a flat surface of a solid figure

D. where two or more faces of a solid figure meet

E. lines that intersect to form four right angles

F. the space between two nonparallel rays that share an endpoint

G. a line with two endpoints

H. lines that never intersect

Read the story. Then, answer the questions.

   Tara found a pair of pink sunglasses on the bus. They had red lightning bolts on the earpieces. Tara liked them. After lunch, she put on the sunglasses to wear at recess. A girl ran to her and said, "Excuse me, but I think those are mine." Tara's heart sank.

13. What do you think Tara will do? _____

_____

14. Which clues helped you decide? _____

_____

Rewrite the paragraph with the correct punctuation and capitalization.

   last summer we went camping in colorado we went hiking and swimming every day one time i actually saw a baby white-tailed deer with spots we also took photos of a lot of pretty rocks flowers and leaves we had a great time i didn't want to leave

_____

_____

_____

_____

_____

_____

_____

Place Value/Geometry

Skill IDs: KSN • X72

DAY 12

Write each number. Then, write its expanded form.

1. five hundred sixty-one _____

2. four thousand eight hundred twenty-six _____

Count how many are in each set. Write each number.

3. _____

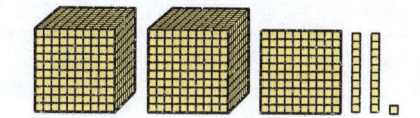

4. _____

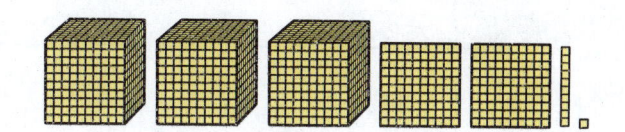

Write the letter of each definition next to the correct geometry term.

5. _____ parallel lines

6. _____ perpendicular lines

7. _____ vertex

8. _____ face

9. _____ edge

10. _____ ray

11. _____ line segment

12. _____ angle

A. line with one endpoint that continues in one direction

B. the endpoint of three line segments on a solid figure

C. a flat surface of a solid figure

D. where two or more faces of a solid figure meet

E. lines that intersect to form four right angles

F. the space between two nonparallel rays that share an endpoint

G. a line with two endpoints

H. lines that never intersect

© Carson Dellosa Education

83

Read the story. Then, answer the questions.

Tara found a pair of pink sunglasses on the bus. They had red lightning bolts on the earpieces. Tara liked them. After lunch, she put on the sunglasses to wear at recess. A girl ran to her and said, "Excuse me, but I think those are mine." Tara's heart sank.

13. What do you think Tara will do? _____

_____

14. Which clues helped you decide? _____

_____

Rewrite the paragraph with the correct punctuation and capitalization.

last summer we went camping in colorado we went hiking and swimming every day one time i actually saw a baby white-tailed deer with spots we also took photos of a lot of pretty rocks flowers and leaves we had a great time i didn't want to leave

_____

_____

_____

_____

_____

_____

Geometry

Use a protractor to measure each angle. Write each angle measurement. Then, write *right*, *straight*, *acute*, or *obtuse* to identify each angle.

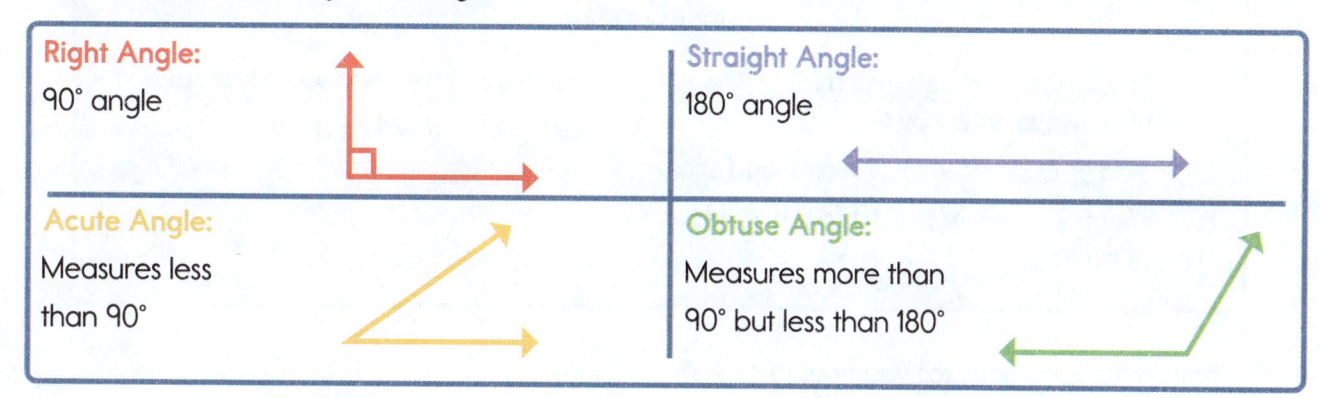

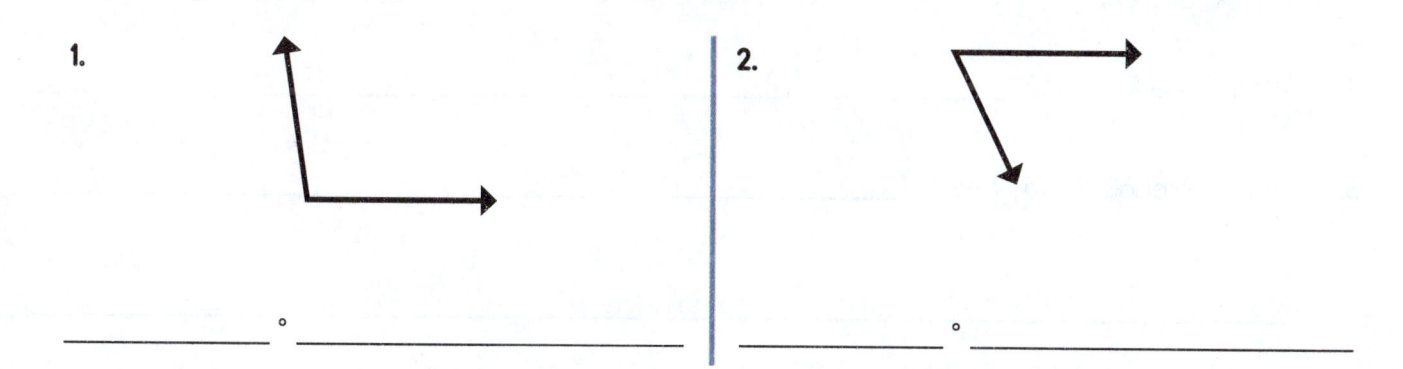

Right Angle: 90° angle	Straight Angle: 180° angle
Acute Angle: Measures less than 90°	Obtuse Angle: Measures more than 90° but less than 180°

1. _____° _____

2. _____° _____

Use a protractor to measure angles *BAC* and *CAD*. Add angles *BAC* and *CAD* together to find the measure of angle *BAD*.

3.

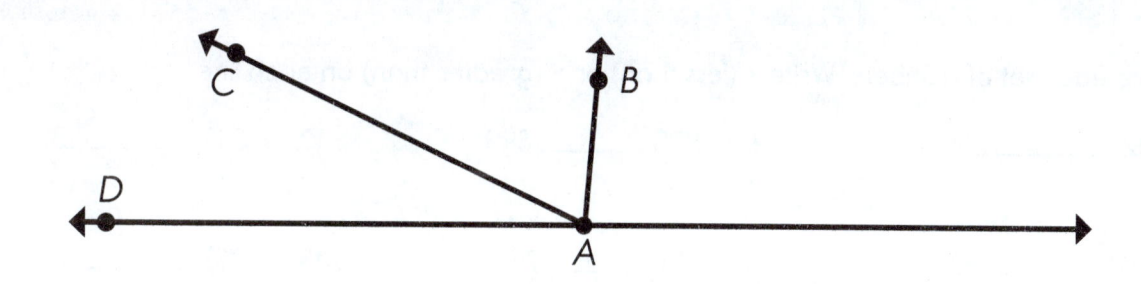

Angle *BAC* = _____° Angle *CAD* = _____°

_____° + _____° = _____°

DAY 13

Reading Comprehension/Numbers

Read the directions from the oatmeal box. Then, answer the questions.

> **Instant Oatmeal**
>
> 1. Empty the package into a microwave-safe bowl.
> 2. Add $\frac{2}{3}$ cup (156 mL) of water and stir.
> 3. Microwave on high for 1 to 2 minutes; and stir.
> 4. Pour some milk on top if desired.
> 5. Let cool; eat with a spoon.

4. What do the directions tell you how to make?

   A. granola   B. instant oatmeal   C. cold oatmeal

5. What is the first step? _____

6. What materials do you need? _____

   _____

7. How long should it take to make this?

   A. a few seconds   B. a few minutes   C. 30 minutes

Compare each set of numbers. Write < (less than) or > (greater than) on each line.

8. 126 _____ 261
9. 999 _____ 899
10. 342 _____ 231

11. 524 _____ 624
12. 619 _____ 719
13. 267 _____ 367

14. 1,638 _____ 738
15. 4,206 _____ 5,206
16. 3,487 _____ 3,748

Let's Play Today *See page 60.

Do 10 squats.

Graphing/Parts of Speech

Skill IDs: B8Q • NHK

DAY 14

Display the data on the line plot.

Plant	A	B	C	D	E	F	G	H	I	J
Inches grown	$\frac{1}{4}$	$\frac{3}{4}$	$\frac{1}{4}$	$\frac{2}{4}$	$\frac{1}{4}$	$\frac{1}{4}$	$\frac{3}{4}$	$\frac{4}{4}$	$\frac{4}{4}$	$\frac{1}{4}$

Key
1 plant = X

[Number line from 0 to $\frac{4}{4}$ with marks at $\frac{1}{4}$, $\frac{2}{4}$, $\frac{3}{4}$, $\frac{4}{4}$]

For plants that grew $\frac{1}{4}$ inch, what was the total number of inches grown? _____

Write a prepositional phrase to complete each sentence. Begin each phrase with a preposition from the box.

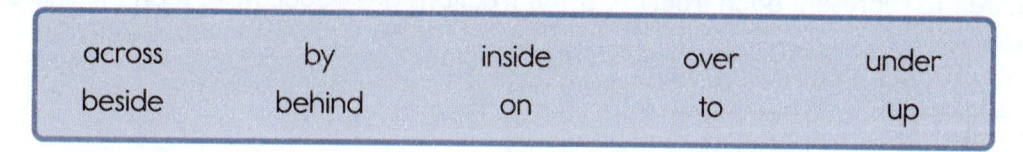

across	by	inside	over	under
beside	behind	on	to	up

1. Maggie found her brother hiding _____ **behind a door** _____.

2. It was hot outside, so we decided to have the picnic _____.

3. Donita's legs were tired from the long hike _____.

4. I left your books _____.

5. Tomas sat _____ in the cafeteria.

6. The cardinal flew _____ and landed on a branch.

DAY 14

Skill IDs: FZ7 • HYC — Search for these skill IDs on IXL.com for more practice!

Language Arts/Fractions

Study the table of contents. Then, answer the questions.

Table of Contents
Communicating with Others 9
Writing a Story. 16
Word Meanings. 20
Following Directions 25
Using Words Correctly 32
Commas 40
Proofreading 53
Describing Words 57

7. On what page should you start reading to learn about writing a story?

   _____

8. On what page should you start reading to learn about commas?

   _____

9. On what page should you start reading to learn how to describe what something looks like?

   _____

Shade the models to represent each fraction. If the fractions are equal, write = on the line. If they are not equal, write ≠.

10. $\frac{1}{4}$ _____ $\frac{4}{8}$

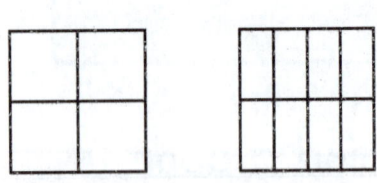

11. $\frac{2}{3}$ _____ $\frac{8}{12}$

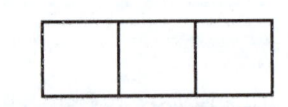

12. $\frac{5}{8}$ _____ $\frac{1}{2}$

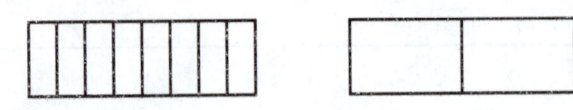

13. $\frac{1}{3}$ _____ $\frac{3}{9}$

88
© Carson Dellosa Education

Problem Solving/Writing

Solve each problem. Show your work.

1. 78 boxes were loaded into a truck. Each box weighed 9 pounds. How many pounds were loaded into the truck?

   _____ pounds

2. A broadcasting tower will be 2,542 feet tall when it is completed. So far, the builders have constructed 1,268 feet of the tower. How many more feet do the builders have to go?

   _____ feet

Write an ending to the story.

The three friends had not seen Logan for a long time. They were standing in the main room of the natural history museum. "He was here a little while ago," said Kim. The museum was closing. Most of the other visitors had already left.

"Logan likes the dinosaur exhibit and the astronomy room," said Craig. "Maybe we should go look there."

Just then, a museum guard said, "Sorry, but the museum is closing. You'll have to come back tomorrow."

_____

_____

_____

_____

_____

DAY 15

Skill IDs: U6P • Z59

Problem Solving/Language Arts

Circle the equation you could use to solve each word problem.

3. A 65-story building is 780 feet tall. How tall is a 42-story building?

   A. (65 − 42) × 780 = ?
   B. (780 ÷ 65) × 42 = ?
   C. (65 × 42) ÷ 780 = ?
   D. (780 ÷ ?) + 42 = 65

4. The McCrary Theater seats 950 people. There are 400 seats in Section B and 350 seats in Section C. The best seats are in Section A. If all tickets for seating in Section A are sold, the theater collects $3,600. How much does it cost per ticket for seating in Section A?

   A. 3,600 ÷ [950 − (400 + 350)] = ?
   B. (400 + 350) × 950 ÷ 3,600 = ?
   C. (3,600 ÷ 950) × (400 + 350) = ?
   D. 3,600 ÷ (950 + 400 + 350) = ?

A simile compares two unlike things using the words *like* or *as*. Complete each sentence by making a comparison.

5. The piano keys were as white as _____snow_____.

6. The fireworks were as bright as the _____.

7. The balloons were like a bunch of _____.

8. Her eyes sparkled like _____.

9. The wind was as gentle as _____.

Fast Fun Fact

The largest balloon sculpture of a landmark was made of a section of the Great Wall of China. It used 103,000 balloons.

Capitalization/Reading Comprehension

Draw three lines beneath each letter that should be capitalized.

Jane Goodall

jane goodall was born in 1934 in hampstead, london. She was given a chimpanzee toy named jubilee when she was young. Jane goodall visited the gombe stream national park in Tanzania to study chimpanzees. She later got a degree from the University of cambridge. jane goodall gave the chimpanzees she studied names like fifi and david Greybeard. She has won many awards, including the united nations messenger of peace prize.

The main idea tells what a story is about. Underline the sentence in each story that tells the main idea.

1. Penny's dog Coco likes to eat special snacks. Coco eats carrots. She also likes cheese. Her favorite snack is peanut butter dog biscuits. Penny makes sure that Coco does not eat too many snacks. They also go for a walk every afternoon.

2. Oliver Owl is teaching Owen Owl to fly. Oliver tells Owen to perch on the highest branch of the tallest tree. "Then, jump and flap your wings as hard as you can," he says. Owen is nervous, but he trusts Oliver. He jumps from the branch and flaps his wings. Oliver cheers as Owen starts to fly! Later, Owen says that Oliver is good at teaching little owls how to fly.

Mindful Moment

What is something that happened today that you are thankful for? Write about it on a separate sheet of paper.

DAY 16

Writing

Skill ID: SJM — Search for this skill ID on IXL.com for more practice!

What is the funniest story you have ever been told? Retell the story. Then, answer the questions.

_____

_____

_____

_____

_____

_____

_____

_____

3. What was the main idea?

_____

_____

4. What would be a good title for the story?

_____

Measurement/Fractions

Skill IDs: YWR · 78D

DAY 17

Write *cm*, *m*, or *km* to complete each sentence.

1 meter (m) = 100 centimeters (cm)	1 kilometer (km) = 1,000 meters (m)

1. Reid is 150 _____ tall.

2. Paige's room is 5 _____ wide.

3. Whitney's hand is 14 _____ long and 5 _____ wide.

4. Mr. Suarez drove his car 84 _____ the first hour.

5. The distance from Chicago, Illinois, to Denver, Colorado, is 1,466 _____.

6. Myla's kitchen is approximately 7 _____ wide.

7. The flagpole at the post office is 46 _____ tall.

8. Lin and Tara walked approximately 3 _____ in 30 minutes.

Compare the fractions. Use the greater than (>), less than (<), or equal to (=) symbols. Hint: It is easier to compare fractions when their denominators are the same.

9. $\frac{3}{4}$ ⎛=⎞ $\frac{9}{12}$

10. $\frac{5}{8}$ ◯ $\frac{1}{4}$

11. $\frac{2}{10}$ ◯ $\frac{1}{2}$

12. $\frac{6}{9}$ ◯ $\frac{1}{3}$

13. $\frac{7}{8}$ ◯ $\frac{5}{8}$

14. $\frac{1}{2}$ ◯ $\frac{7}{10}$

15. $\frac{4}{12}$ ◯ $\frac{3}{4}$

16. $\frac{3}{6}$ ◯ $\frac{2}{3}$

17. $\frac{7}{8}$ ◯ $\frac{3}{4}$

18. $\frac{1}{6}$ ◯ $\frac{1}{12}$

19. $\frac{3}{9}$ ◯ $\frac{1}{3}$

20. $\frac{2}{5}$ ◯ $\frac{5}{10}$

© Carson Dellosa Education

DAY 17

Skill IDs: Z46 • TXS

Problem Solving/Reading Comprehension

Write an equation to solve each word problem.

21. Sondra read 4 books. Lucas read 5 times as many books. How many books did Lucas read?

22. For most of the year, a florist sells 7 dozen roses per week. During the week of Valentine's Day, she sells 133 dozen roses. How many times more is this amount than the usual weekly sale?

Read the story. Then, answer the questions.

The children were playing baseball in the empty lot. Brooke was at bat. She swung hard and hit the ball farther than anyone else that day. The ball sailed across the lot and smashed through Ms. Havel's window. Brooke knew that Ms. Havel would be upset. The other children scattered and ran for home. Brooke looked at the broken window. Then, she started walking toward the house.

23. What do you think Brooke will do? _____

_____

24. Which clues helped you decide? _____

_____

Fractions/Parts of Speech

Solve each equation. Shade the models to help you.

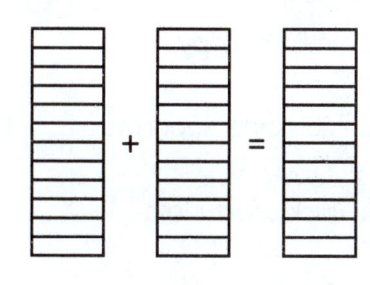

1. $\frac{5}{12} + \frac{2}{12} =$ _____

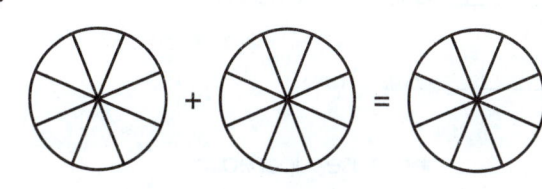

2. $\frac{3}{8} + \frac{4}{8} =$ _____

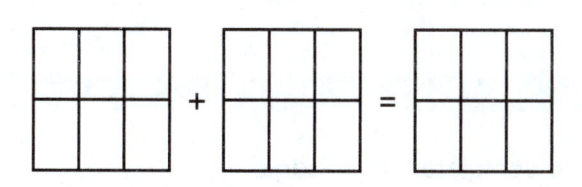

3. $\frac{3}{6} + \frac{1}{6} =$ _____

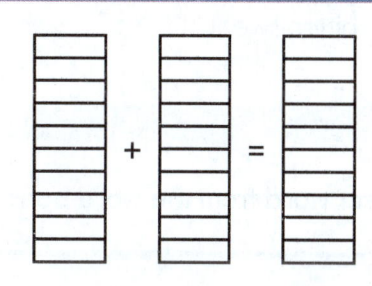

4. $\frac{4}{10} + \frac{5}{10} =$ _____

A relative pronoun is used to begin a phrase that describes a noun. Some relative pronouns are *that*, *which*, and *who*. Circle the relative pronoun in each sentence below. Then, write two sentences that use relative pronouns.

5. The twins who live next door are nine years old.

6. My aunt, who lives in California, has invited me to visit during spring break.

7. Your e-mail, which I received yesterday, was really thoughtful.

8. The birds that nested in the fern have finally laid eggs.

9. _____

10. _____

DAY 18

Vocabulary

Read each pair of words. If they are synonyms, write *S* on the line. If they are antonyms, write *A*.

11. _____ ancient, modern
12. _____ imitate, copy
13. _____ assist, help
14. _____ combine, separate
15. _____ increase, decrease
16. _____ lucky, fortunate
17. _____ enlarge, magnify
18. _____ frequent, seldom
19. _____ accept, refuse
20. _____ patient, impatient
21. _____ bitter, sweet
22. _____ genuine, real

Write the correct word from the word bank on each line to complete the passage.

| plant | heat | sunlight | Earth | oxygen | plants |

Sunlight is very important to our planet, _____. Most of our food comes from _____ life. _____ also give off the _____ we breathe. Without _____, plants would die, and we would not have food or air. The _____ of the sun also warms Earth. Without it, we would freeze.

Let's Play Today *See page 60.

Play tug-of-war. Tie pieces of fabric together to make a rope. Mark a line on the ground. Have two teams start pulling on the rope at the same time until one team pulls the other across the line!

Add., Subt., Mult. & Div./Vocabulary

Solve each problem.

1. 2)224

2. 16
   × 7

3. 3)156

4. 46
   − 28

5. 38
   + 17

6. 57
   + 34

7. 18
   × 4

8. 24
   × 7

9. 7)770

10. 804
    − 238

11. 132
    − 78

12. 176
    + 394

Homophones are words that sound the same but have different meanings and are spelled differently. Write the correct homophone from the parentheses to complete each sentence.

13. I have _____ more days of school. (to, two)

14. Have you _____ this book before? (read, red)

15. I like that song _____. (two, too)

16. _____ is my favorite color. (Red, Read)

17. We are going _____ Lake Louise this summer. (to, two)

Fractions/Word Study

Add to find each sum. Write each answer in its simplest form.

18. $\frac{1}{3} + \frac{2}{3} =$

19. $\frac{4}{5} + \frac{5}{6} =$

20. $\frac{1}{6} + \frac{1}{6} =$

21. $\frac{3}{6} + \frac{1}{6} =$

22. $\frac{2}{4} + \frac{2}{4} =$

23. $\frac{1}{2} + \frac{1}{2} =$

24. $\frac{5}{8} + \frac{3}{8} =$

25. $\frac{5}{5} + \frac{2}{5} =$

26. $\frac{2}{10} + \frac{4}{10} =$

Write each word from the word bank under the correct heading.

| buttermilk | snowstorm | replanted | peaceful | daylight |
| airplane | selection | sleepless | football | unpacked |

Compound Words   Words with Prefixes or Suffixes

_____   _____

_____   _____

_____   _____

_____   _____

_____   _____

Reading Comprehension

Read the passage. Then, answer the questions.

Flash Floods

Rain is good for people and plants. When it rains too much, though, people can be in danger. A flash flood occurs when a lot of rain falls quickly, filling the streets faster than the water can drain. Driving is very dangerous in a flash flood. A person's car could be swept away. If you live in an area where flash flooding is likely, you should listen to radio or TV news reports when it starts to rain. Be ready to leave your home with your family if a newscaster says to move to higher ground. If you leave on foot, do not walk through moving water. You should not drive through standing water unless it is less than 6 inches (15.24 centimeters) deep. After a flood, listen to news reports. A newscaster will tell you when you can return home safely and when the water from your tap will be safe to drink.

1. What is the main idea of this passage?

   A. Flash floods can be dangerous and occur suddenly.

   B. Never drive through a flooded area.

   C. Take important items with you when you leave your home.

2. What happens during a flash flood? _____

   _____

3. What could happen to a car in a flash flood? _____

   _____

4. What should you do when it starts to rain? _____

   _____

5. How does the author support the idea that flash floods are dangerous to people?

   _____

DAY 20

Fractions/Spelling

Solve each equation. Shade the models to help you.

6.

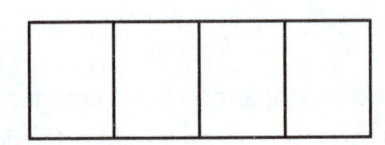

$3 \times \frac{1}{4} =$ _____

7.

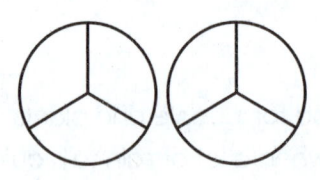

$5 \times \frac{1}{3} =$ _____

8.

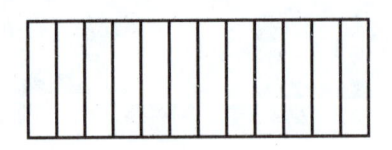

$4 \times \frac{3}{12} =$ _____

9.

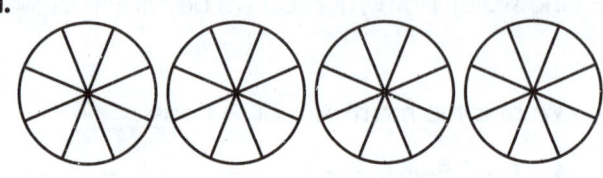

$6 \times \frac{5}{8} =$ _____

Circle each correctly spelled word. Then, write it in the blank to complete each sentence.

10. I took a _____ of the baby panda at the zoo.

pickture   picture   pecture   pikture

11. The _____ children helped their mother rake leaves.

thotful   toughtful   thoughtful   thowghtful

12. You need to remember to keep your doctor's _____.

apointment   apowntment   appointment   appointtment

Fast Fun Fact

A panda's diet is almost entirely bamboo leaves. They eat from 26–84 pounds (12–38 kilograms) of bamboo a day!

Science Experiment

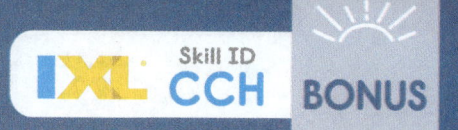

Bounce Away!

How much height does a ball lose with each bounce?

Energy is the ability to do work. Potential energy is the energy that an object has because of its position. The energy of an object in motion is called kinetic energy. If you hold a tennis ball above the ground, it has potential energy due to its position. When the ball is released, gravity pulls it down. The ball's potential energy becomes kinetic energy as it falls.

Materials:

- meterstick
- tennis ball

Procedure:

Hold the meterstick vertically with one end against the floor. Hold the tennis ball so that the bottom is at the zero mark.

Drop the ball from a height of 1 meter. Watch carefully to determine the height of the first, second, and third bounces. Round the answer to the nearest centimeter, and record the information in the table below.

Because of the speed at which the ball bounces, you may want to ask another person to help you measure the height of the ball's bounces.

Bounce	Height of Bounce
1	
2	
3	

What's This All About?
The shape of the tennis ball changes slightly when it hits the floor. Some energy is lost as heat (due to friction from air resistance) and when the ball changes shape. Because of the lost energy, the ball will not bounce to the same height it was dropped from. After the ball hits the ground, it returns to its original shape. The energy becomes upward motion as the ball bounces into the air.

Think About It
How are potential and kinetic energy different?

© Carson Dellosa Education

Separating Salt and Pepper*

How can a mixture of salt and pepper be separated?

Some mixtures are homogeneous. This means that they combine evenly. For example, when you mix sugar and water, you get sugar water. The sugar spreads evenly throughout the water.

If you mix sand and water, you get a heterogeneous mixture. The sand sinks to the bottom and will not stay mixed with the water.

In this experiment, determine whether salt and pepper is a homogeneous or heterogeneous mixture.

Materials:

- balance or kitchen scale
- pepper
- tray
- balloon
- salt
- your hair (clean and dry)

Procedure:

Use the balance or scale to weigh several teaspoons of salt and pepper. Then, mix the salt and pepper on the tray. Gently shake the tray so that the mixture forms a single layer. Then, blow up the balloon.

Keep your hand in the same place on the balloon and rub the other side of the balloon back and forth about 20 times on your clean, dry hair. Then, hold the balloon about 1 inch (2.5 centimeters) above the mixture of salt and pepper. The pepper will be attracted to the balloon. Most of the salt will stay where it is.

Pour the remaining mixture onto the balance or scale. Measure the mixture again to find its mass. Record your data in the table.

Trial	Amount of Salt Placed in Mixture	Amount of Salt Remaining in Mixture
1		
2		
3		

Is the mixture of salt and pepper homogeneous or heterogeneous? _____

*See page 2.

Social Studies Activity

BONUS

Lines of Latitude

Lines of latitude are imaginary lines that run east to west on a map. They are marked in degrees (°) and help people locate places around the world. The equator is the line at 0° latitude. The lines of latitude on the map below are measured in 20° segments from the equator. Places north of the equator have the letter *N* after their degrees. Places south of the equator have the letter *S* after their degrees.

Study the map. Then, answer the questions.

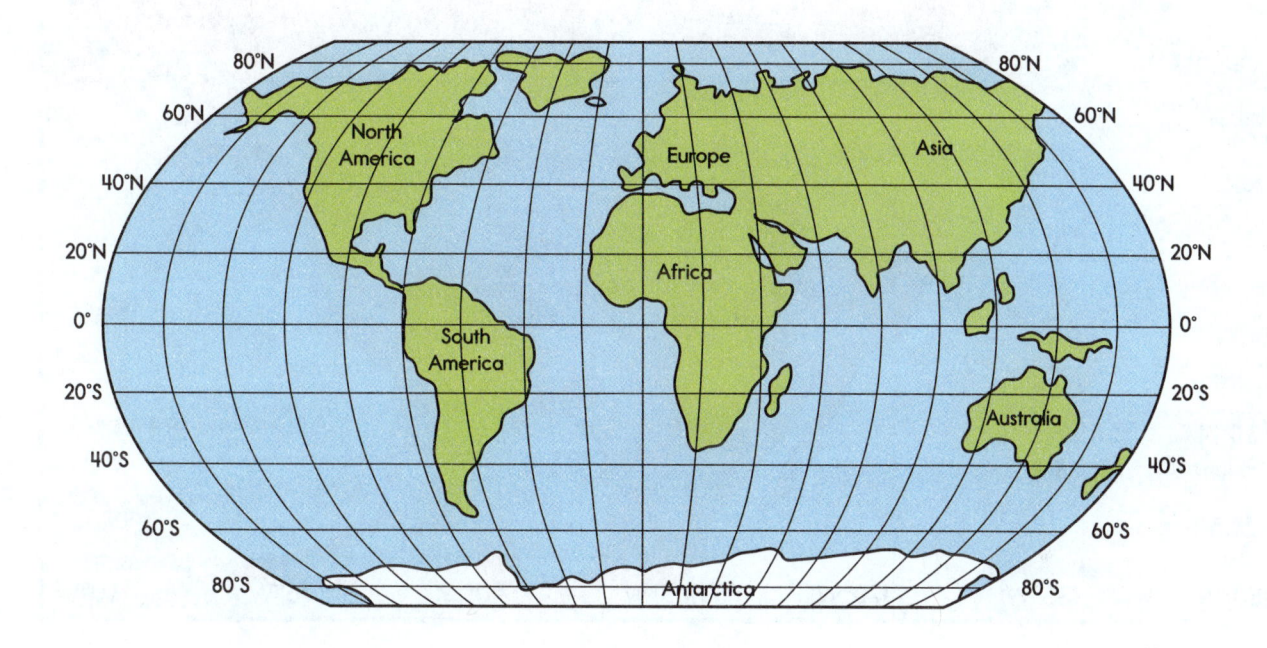

1. The equator is at _____° latitude.

2. For locations in North America, the latitude should be followed by the letter _____.

3. The latitude for the southern tip of South America would be followed by the letter _____.

4. Use a red crayon or marker to trace the equator.

© Carson Dellosa Education

103

Latitude and Longitude

Use the map to find the cities located at each latitude and longitude. Then, write the name of each city.

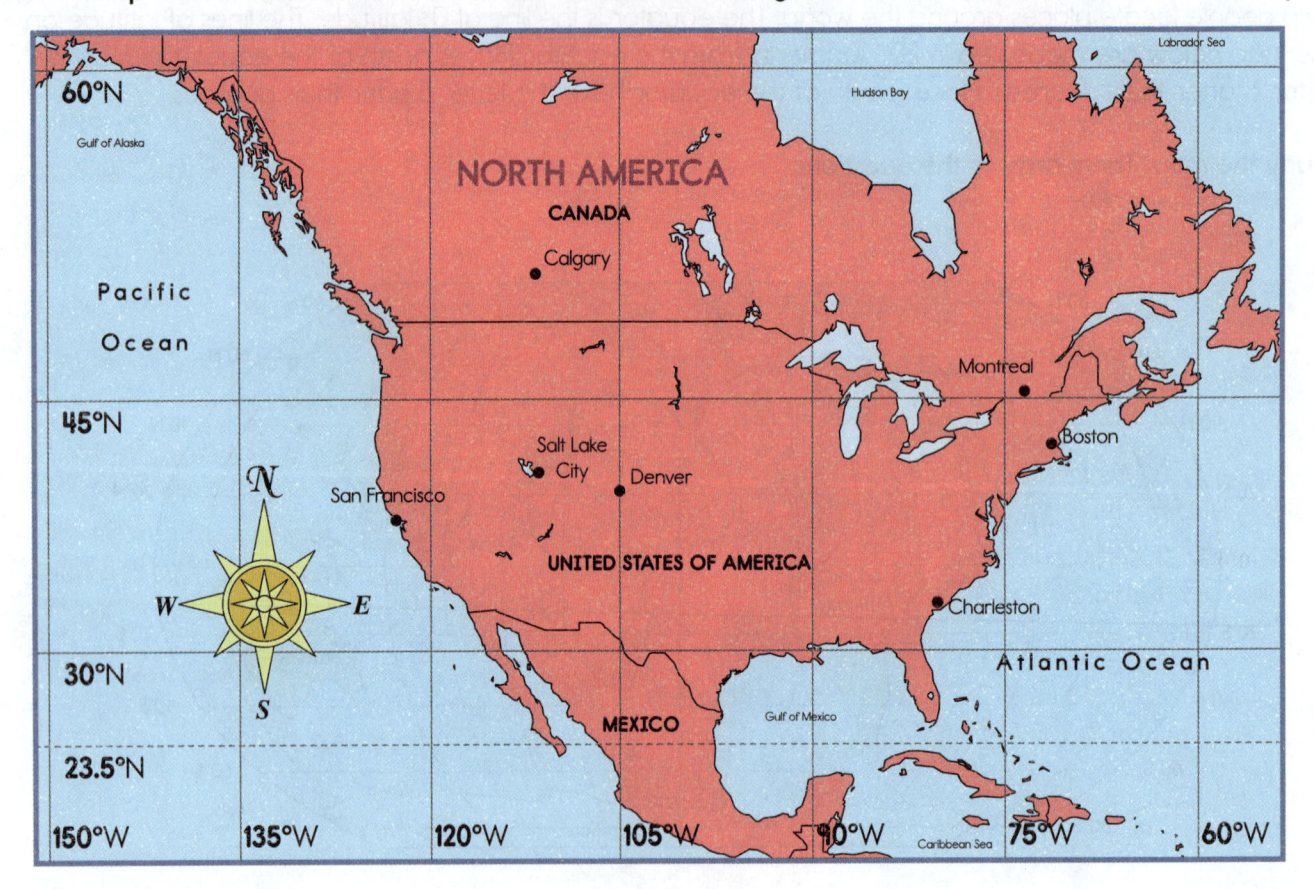

	Latitude	Longitude	City
1.	51°N	114°W	_____
2.	39°N	105°W	_____
3.	42°N	71°W	_____
4.	32°N	79°W	_____
5.	45°N	73°W	_____
6.	40°N	111°W	_____
7.	37°N	122°W	_____

Social Studies Activity

BONUS

Coat of Arms

A coat of arms is a design that belongs to a particular person or family. The colors, symbols, and backgrounds used in a coat of arms all have special meanings and say something about the coat of arms's owner. For example, the color blue may represent truth and loyalty, while a lion may represent courage.

Create a coat of arms. Think of some qualities that you have and are proud of. Brainstorm ways that you could represent those qualities on your coat of arms. Go online with an adult if you need more information. Then, draw your coat of arms in the box.

SECTION 3

Monthly Goals

Think of three goals to set for yourself this month. For example, you may want to exercise for 20 minutes each day. Write your goals on the lines and review them with an adult.

Place a sticker next to each of your goals that you complete. Feel proud that you have met your goals!

1. _____ | PLACE STICKER |

2. _____ | PLACE STICKER |

3. _____ | PLACE STICKER |

Word List

The following words are used in this section. Read each word. Use a dictionary to look up each word that you do not know. Then, write two sentences. Use a word from the word list in each sentence.

central	rely
ecosystem	rural
interviewing	statue
murmuring	urban
organized	vapor

4. _____

_____

5. _____

_____

Introduction to Endurance

This section includes Let's Play Today and Mindful Moments activities that focus on endurance. These activities are designed to help you develop mental and physical stamina. If you have limited mobility, feel free to modify any suggested activity or choose a different one from the list on the following page.

Let's Play Today

Many children seem to have endless energy and can run, jump, and play for hours. But endurance does not come naturally to everyone. Developing endurance requires regular exercise that gets the body moving and the heart pumping, like arm punches, jumping jacks, dancing, and playing sports.

Make exercise a part of your everyday routine during the summer. Do things that make you breathe harder and move your body, such as playing hopscotch, going for a walk, kicking a ball with someone, climbing on playground equipment, riding a bike, and more.

Mindful Moments

Endurance means to stick with something, and it applies to the mind as well as to the body. If you have ever felt like giving up at something but instead you persevered and finished the task, you demonstrated endurance.

Think of a time when you wanted to quit a task. Maybe you didn't like the new game you were playing or the new skill you were practicing, and so you wanted to quit. What did you do? Realize that it often takes a while to learn something new. If you quit instead of persevering through a challenge, you wouldn't learn how to do new things and you wouldn't grow as a person. Endurance and perseverance build character and make people mentally strong. Quitting should be a last resort. Developing endurance at a young age will help you persevere through challenging physical and mental activities you encounter in life.

Engaging Online Practice

Bring learning to life with fun, interactive activities on IXL! Look for the Skill ID box and type the 3-digit code into the search bar on IXL.com or the IXL mobile app. Ten questions per day are free!

IXL Skill IDs: 5UN • D9K

SECTION 3

Let's Play Today

Get up and moving with these Let's Play Today activities. Section 3 focuses on endurance. Endurance is being able to complete many repetitions of a task, such as 10 jumping jacks, or perform an activity for an extended amount of time, such as riding a bike for 10 minutes. Building endurance will help you get through everyday tasks and find success with physical activities and sports. Use this list in addition to or as a replacement for any Let's Play Today suggestions on the activity pages. This list was developed to be inclusive of a variety of abilities. Choose the ones that are a good fit for you! Make modifications as needed. Some activities may require adult supervision. See page 2 for full caution information.

Jump Rope:
Start by jumping rope for 30 seconds. Jump rope every day and try to increase the amount of time you can jump every day.

Freeze Dance:
Have one person control the music. Ask them to play a favorite song. Move your body to the music while it plays. When the music pauses, stop moving. If you move after the music stops, the person controlling the music assigns an endurance challenge (5 jumping jacks, push-ups, etc.). Then you can rejoin the game.

Scavenger Hunt Hike:
Go on a scavenger hunt hike. Create a list of things you think you might see, such as a traffic light, a dog, or a particular type of flower. Cross items off your list as you go. You can also build endurance by going on a simple walk or run.

Fun on Wheels:
Go on a bike ride or play bike games. This works great with wheelchairs too. Create an obstacle course of cones and weave in and out, challenge a friend to a race, or use chalk to create roads, stop signs, and more.

Let's Go Team:
Playing team sports is a great way to build endurance. Basketball, soccer, football, softball, baseball, volleyball, and more are all great ways to improve endurance. Choose a favorite team sport and get a group of kids together to play at a local park.

Multiplication/Reading Comprehension

Multiply to find each product.

1. 26 × 12
2. 49 × 33
3. 87 × 28
4. 51 × 42
5. 94 × 78

6. 81 × 32
7. 23 × 18
8. 55 × 37
9. 62 × 29
10. 75 × 46

Read the paragraph. Then, answer the questions.

  Sandra's mother offered to help her get ready for the new school year. Like a lot of kids, Sandra grew over the summer. She grew a full inch taller! Her shoes were too tight, and her pants were almost above her ankles.

11. What do you think Sandra and her mother will do? _____

_____

12. Which clues helped you decide? _____

_____

Mindful Moment

What is the hardest task you have ever completed? How did you feel when it was over? On a separate sheet of paper, write a paragraph about your experience.

DAY 1

IXL Skill ID RTE — Search for this skill ID on IXL.com for more practice!

Subtraction/Spelling

Complete the table.

	Total Price	Amount Given to Clerk	Change Received
13.	$1.35	$1.50	$0.15
14.	$2.50	$5.00	
15.	$0.95	$1.00	
16.	$1.80	$2.00	
17.	$6.42	$10.00	
18.	$9.35	$20.00	
19.	$5.55	$6.00	
20.	$13.95	$20.00	
21.	$85.00	$100.00	

Underline the correct spelling of each word.

22. decieve   deceive
23. accompany   acompany
24. exersise   exercise
25. sincerely   sincerley
26. particular   particuler

27. patiunt   patient
28. friend   freind
29. becuse   because
30. guard   garde
31. although   althouh

Reading Comprehension

Read the passage. Then, answer the questions.

Food Webs

A food web is a drawing that shows how different living things are connected. In a food web, the living things at the bottom are eaten by the animals directly above them. For example, a food web might start at the bottom with plants. Plants do not eat other living things. Above these plants might be small animals, such as mice, that eat plants. Larger animals, such as owls and snakes, eat mice. A food web can tell us what might happen if certain plants or animals disappear from an **ecosystem**, or the surroundings in which all of the plants and animals live. In the food web described above, if something happened to the plants, then the mice would not have as much food. This would affect the owls and snakes, who would also not have enough food. Soon, there would be fewer of each type of animal. This is why it is important to protect all living things in an ecosystem, not just the larger ones.

1. What is the main idea of this passage?

    A. Food webs show how all living things are connected.

    B. Owls and snakes are the most important animals.

    C. Only the animals at the top of the food web should be protected.

2. What is a food web? _____

    _____

3. What is an *ecosystem*?

    A. a food web for very large animals

    B. the surroundings where a group of plants and animals live

    C. a place where only plants grow

4. How does the author support the idea that it is important to protect all living things in an ecosystem?

    _____

    _____

DAY 2

Measurement

Find each equivalent measurement.

> 2 cups = 1 pint
> 2 pints = 1 quart
> 4 quarts = 1 gallon
> 16 cups = 1 gallon

5. 5 quarts = _____ pints

6. 3 gallons = _____ pints

7. 4 cups = _____ pints

8. 2 pints = _____ cups

9. _____ gallons = 16 pints

10. 5 gallons = _____ quarts

11. _____ pints = 2 quarts

12. 3 quarts = _____ cups

Solve each word problem.

13. Kennan is making soup. The recipe calls for 2 quarts of broth. How many cups of broth does Kennan need?

14. An ice-cream shop sold 8 quarts of ice cream. How many gallons did they sell?

Language Arts & Writing

Skill IDs
LJX • XJV

DAY 3

Do you think schools should schedule two recesses each day? Why or why not? Support your opinion with facts and reasons and include a conclusion.

_____

_____

_____

_____

_____

_____

Read each sentence. Write *F* if it is a fact. Write *O* if it is an opinion.

1. __F__ Abraham Lincoln was the 16th president of the United States.

2. _____ Spring is the best time of the year.

3. _____ Chocolate cake is the best dessert in the world.

4. _____ Daytime and nighttime depend on the position of the sun in the sky.

5. _____ Dogs are the best pets.

6. _____ Neil Armstrong walked on the moon in 1969.

7. _____ Lava rock was once hot liquid.

8. _____ Eating too much candy is bad for your teeth.

9. _____ Everyone should like chocolate ice cream.

10. _____ Reading is the best way to spend a rainy day.

DAY 3

Reading Comprehension

Read the passage. Then, answer the questions.

Edward Murrow

Edward Murrow was an American journalist. He became famous during World War II. Murrow was born in 1908 in North Carolina. After college, he began working for a radio station. Many Americans listened to his live broadcasts during the bombing of London, England, in September 1939. Before Murrow's reports, people in the United States learned about the war through newsreels in movie theaters or articles in newspapers. Now, they could learn about the war in London as it was happening. After the war, Murrow worked as a reporter in radio and then in television. He became known for interviewing, or asking questions of, important people. Other newscasters followed in Murrow's footsteps. Today, we still rely on reporters in other countries for news and information. And, we still listen to reporters' conversations with famous people.

11. What is the main idea of this passage?

   A. Edward Murrow was a brave American journalist.

   B. Edward Murrow talked to many famous people.

   C. Edward Murrow worked in London.

12. How did people learn about the war before Murrow's reports? _____

_____

13. Write a brief summary of the passage. _____

_____

14. How did Murrow change the way journalists work? _____

_____

Let's Play Today *See page 108.

Have an animal race! Mark a finish line, and then choose a type of animal walk to race to the finish, such as the crab walk or bear crawl.

Language Arts & Writing

Skill IDs: LJX • XJV

DAY 3

Do you think schools should schedule two recesses each day? Why or why not? Support your opinion with facts and reasons and include a conclusion.

_____

_____

_____

_____

_____

Read each sentence. Write *F* if it is a fact. Write *O* if it is an opinion.

1. __F__ Abraham Lincoln was the 16th president of the United States.

2. _____ Spring is the best time of the year.

3. _____ Chocolate cake is the best dessert in the world.

4. _____ Daytime and nighttime depend on the position of the sun in the sky.

5. _____ Dogs are the best pets.

6. _____ Neil Armstrong walked on the moon in 1969.

7. _____ Lava rock was once hot liquid.

8. _____ Eating too much candy is bad for your teeth.

9. _____ Everyone should like chocolate ice cream.

10. _____ Reading is the best way to spend a rainy day.

© Carson Dellosa Education

113

DAY 3

Reading Comprehension

Read the passage. Then, answer the questions.

Edward Murrow

Edward Murrow was an American journalist. He became famous during World War II. Murrow was born in 1908 in North Carolina. After college, he began working for a radio station. Many Americans listened to his live broadcasts during the bombing of London, England, in September 1939. Before Murrow's reports, people in the United States learned about the war through newsreels in movie theaters or articles in newspapers. Now, they could learn about the war in London as it was happening. After the war, Murrow worked as a reporter in radio and then in television. He became known for interviewing, or asking questions of, important people. Other newscasters followed in Murrow's footsteps. Today, we still rely on reporters in other countries for news and information. And, we still listen to reporters' conversations with famous people.

11. What is the main idea of this passage?

   A. Edward Murrow was a brave American journalist.

   B. Edward Murrow talked to many famous people.

   C. Edward Murrow worked in London.

12. How did people learn about the war before Murrow's reports? _____

   _____

13. Write a brief summary of the passage. _____

   _____

14. How did Murrow change the way journalists work? _____

   _____

Let's Play Today *See page 108.

Have an animal race! Mark a finish line, and then choose a type of animal walk to race to the finish, such as the crab walk or bear crawl.

Multiplication/Measurement

Write factor pairs for each number.

1. 12

___ × ___
___ × ___
___ × ___

2. 15

___ × ___
___ × ___

3. 36

___ × ___
___ × ___
___ × ___
___ × ___
___ × ___

4. 24

___ × ___
___ × ___
___ × ___
___ × ___

5. 28

___ × ___
___ × ___
___ × ___

6. 32

___ × ___
___ × ___
___ × ___

Complete each sentence by writing *more than*, *less than*, or *equal to*.

| 2 cups = 1 pint | 2 pints = 1 quart | 4 quarts = 1 gallon |

7. 2 pints are _____ 1 quart.

8. 3 cups are _____ 1 quart.

9. 1 pint is _____ 1 quart.

10. 1 gallon is _____ 1 pint.

11. 3 quarts are _____ 1 gallon.

12. 2 pints are _____ 4 cups.

DAY 4

Language Arts/Numbers

Sometimes formal language is needed, and sometimes informal language is appropriate. Read each pair of sentences. Write *I* next to sentences with informal language, and *F* next to those with formal language.

13. _____ Earth is home to approximately 4,000 types of cockroaches.

    _____ This is totally unbelievable, but there are about 4,000 different kinds of cockroaches!

14. _____ See ya later!

    _____ I look forward to seeing you again soon.

15. _____ It's been a pleasure to speak with you.

    _____ Nice talking to you.

Continue each counting pattern.

16. 0   3   6   9   12   ____   ____   ____   24   ____

17. 6   12   18   24   ____   ____   ____   48   ____

18. 12   16   20   24   ____   ____   ____   44   ____

19. 33   30   27   24   ____   ____   ____   9   ____

20. 100 98   96   94   ____   ____   ____   86   ____

Reading Comprehension/Fractions

Read the story. Then, answer the questions.

Ivy's grandmother will celebrate her 70th birthday soon. Ivy wants to get her grandmother a special gift, but she spent her money on new books instead. Ivy loves reading about Mexico. Her grandmother came from Mexico, and she read to Ivy when Ivy was little. Lately, her grandmother's eyesight has been failing, so she can no longer see the words on the page.

1. What do you think Ivy will do? _____

_____

2. Which clues helped you decide? _____

_____

Fractions that have a denominator of 10 can also be written as decimals. Write each fraction and/or decimal.

3. [bar model] $\frac{6}{10}$ or 0.6

4. [bar model] ____ or ____

5. [bar model] ____ or ____

6. [bar model] ____ or ____

7. [bar model] ____ or ____

8. [bar model] ____ or ____

9. $\frac{3}{10}$ or ____

10. $1\frac{7}{10}$ or ____

11. $3\frac{5}{10}$ or ____

12. 1.9 or ____

13. 0.8 or ____

14. 3.4 or ____

DAY 5 — Parts of Speech

Skill IDs: 57U • TM8 — Search for these skill IDs on IXL.com for more practice!

Read each set of adjectives in parentheses ( ). Decide what order they should be in to describe the object. Rewrite the words in that order, as shown in the example.

15. hat (black large fuzzy) _____large fuzzy black hat_____

16. teacup (pink small) _____

17. sweater (gray wool cozy) _____

18. trucks (three yellow plastic large) _____

19. salad (Greek fresh small) _____

20. snake (striped venomous) _____

Complete each phrase with an adjective from the box.

| four | blue | sticky | helpful |

21. The treefrog's _____ feet help it climb.

22. There are _____ cookies left.

23. My teacher was _____.

24. I saw a _____ bird on the bird feeder.

Fast Fun Fact

The chocolate chip cookie was created by Ruth Wakefield in 1938. She ran a restaurant called Toll House. She let Nestlé use the recipe and the Toll House name!

© Carson Dellosa Education

Vocabulary/Fractions

DAY 6

IXL Skill IDs: **WZZ • SLQ**

Read the story. Then, write the meaning of each word.

Gabe lives in a large city with his grandparents. The building that he and his grandparents live in is very tall and has different sets of rooms for each family that lives there. This building is called an apartment building. In this community, all of the buildings are close together. People do not have to go far to get things they need in this urban area. Gabe's cousin, Jasper, lives in a rural, or country, community. He plays in his large backyard instead of in a park like Gabe. There is a lot of space between houses where Jasper lives. Both Gabe's and Jasper's neighborhoods have schools, hospitals, and stores.

1. community _____

_____

2. urban _____

_____

3. rural _____

_____

Subtract to find each difference. Write the answers in simplest form.

4. $\frac{2}{6} - \frac{1}{6} =$

5. $\frac{5}{10} - \frac{3}{10} =$

6. $\frac{3}{4} - \frac{2}{4} =$

7. $6\frac{8}{10}$
   $-3\frac{4}{10}$

8. $8\frac{4}{10}$
   $-3\frac{3}{10}$

9. $7\frac{2}{15}$
   $-3\frac{1}{15}$

Mindful Moment

Think about what you would say to a friend if they told you, "I can't do this." How would you encourage them to accomplish their goal?

Reading Comprehension

Read the journal entries and answer the questions that follow.

July 14, 1935

I am almost too tired tonight to write. The days seem to stretch on forever. Before dawn, we're up to do the milking. I make mush for breakfast nearly every day. We are weary of mush, though I know I should be grateful to have it.

We grow most of our own food, but the harvests are hard work. I wish we had more help, but we can barely pay the hired hands we already have.

President Roosevelt says this Depression will not last forever. Is he right? The most important thing is that we do not lose this farm. "You worry too much for a girl your age, Elizabeth," says Mama. It is hard not to worry in these times.

August 8, 1935

We are so lucky to live in a place where people have such generous spirits. Del Landon from up the road helped Sam fix the holes in the fence. Mrs. Carson brought us fruit preserves and a bag of outgrown clothes.

The best news of all is that we'll have help with our harvest. "Many hands make light work," Pa says, and he's right. When it's time for their crops to come in, we'll help our neighbors, too. Folks need to rely on each other. We'll make it through. I know we will. Better times must be ahead.

10. Tell what you know about Elizabeth's character based on her journal entries. _____

_____

11. What does the saying "Many hands make light work" mean? _____

_____

12. From what point of view is this story told? How does the point of view add to the story?

_____

120   © Carson Dellosa Education

Measurement/Reading Comprehension

Find each equivalent measurement.

> 1 centimeter = 10 millimeters
> 1 meter = 100 centimeters
> 1 kilometer = 1,000 meters

1. 15 meters = _____ centimeters

2. _____ centimeters = 250 millimeters

3. 1 meter = _____ millimeters

4. _____ kilometer = 500 meters

5. 3,000 millimeters = _____ meters

6. 15,000 meters = _____ kilometers

In each sentence, underline the cause and circle the effect.

7. The sky became cloudy, then it started to snow.

8. The temperature dropped overnight, so frost covered the windows.

9. The falling snowflakes made my cheeks wet and cold.

10. Snow stuck to my mittens because I had made a snowman.

11. The snowman melted from the heat of the sun.

12. I swam so long in the pool that I had to put on more sunscreen.

13. Cayce missed the bus because she overslept.

14. Because Shay watched a scary movie on TV, she could not fall asleep.

DAY 7

Writing/Fractions

Imagine that a famous person has come to visit you at home. Who is it? What do you talk about? What are they like? Write a narrative that tells about your experience with this person. Be sure to use descriptive details. Include some dialogue in your writing.

_____

_____

_____

_____

_____

Compare the decimal numbers. Use the greater than (>), less than (<), or equal to (=) symbols.

15. 0.25 ◯ 2.50

16. 0.09 ◯ 0.19

17. 1.50 ◯ 1.05

18. 0.45 ◯ 0.5

19. 3.3 ◯ 0.33

20. 0.52 ◯ 0.05

21. 1.10 ◯ 0.11

22. 0.79 ◯ 0.8

23. 0.45 ◯ 4.50

24. 0.20 ◯ 0.2

25. 5.87 ◯ 7.58

26. 0.45 ◯ 0.54

Reading Comprehension

Read the story. Then, answer the questions.

Planning a City

What do the streets in your city look like? Some cities have streets that are very straight and organized. It is easy to get from one point in the city to another. Other cities have streets that seem to go nowhere. It may be difficult to give directions to your home.

In the past, when a group of people moved to a place and started planning the streets, some of them used a grid system. One example of this is found in the city of Philadelphia, Pennsylvania, which is divided into four sections around a central square. The map was laid out by William Penn in 1682. The grid included wide streets that were easy for people to walk down. Penn left London, England, after a fire destroyed most of the city. London had a maze of narrow streets that were hard to travel on safely. Penn wanted to make sure that people could get around easily and safely. Many other people followed Penn's ideas when setting up their new cities' street systems.

1. What is the main idea of this passage?

    A. William Penn drew the first grid system.

    B. Planning a city is important for safety and ease of use.

    C. Some streets are straight and organized.

2. What is one good thing about having straight streets? _____

    _____

3. What is a grid system?

    A. a plan for developing a city's streets

    B. an area of the classroom

    C. a type of test

4. When did Penn leave London? _____

    _____

5. How are Philadelphia's streets different from London's? _____

    _____

DAY 8

Geometry/Word Study

A figure is symmetrical if it can be folded in half so that the two parts are congruent. Draw one line of symmetry for each figure.

6.

7.

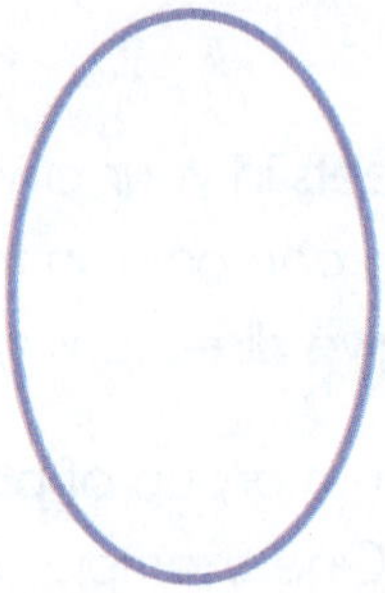

8.

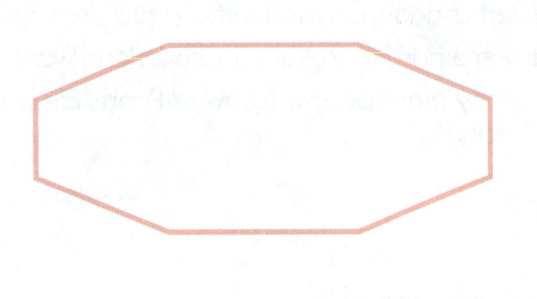

9.

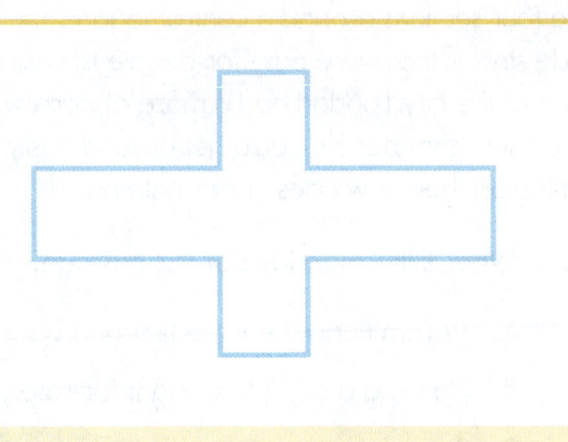

Unscramble the words in parentheses to complete each analogy.

10. *Pillows* are to *soft* as *boards* are to _____. (rdha)

11. *Bells* are to *ring* as *car horns* are to _____. (nkho)

12. *Hear* is to *ears* as *touch* is to _____. (serinfg)

13. *Star* is to *pointed* as *circle* is to _____. (dunor)

14. *Fish* is to *swim* as *bird* is to _____. (ylf)

15. *Elephant* is to *large* as *mouse* is to _____. (malsl)

Let's Play Today *See page 108.

Hop on your right or left foot for 30 seconds.

Problem Solving/Writing

Use the table to answer each question.

Student Music Lesson Schedule

Day 1 (new students only)	Day 2	Day 3	Day 4	Day 5
Nicole	José	Solina	Greg	Jamie
Naomi	Kira	Jamie	Kipley	Solina
Tanya	Kipley	Greg	Jacob	Rebecca
Michelle	Mark	Rebecca	José	Mark
Fiora	Jacob	Margaret	Kira	Drake

1. Other than Jacob, who has a lesson on day 4? _____

2. Tanya, Naomi, and Fiora all have a lesson on which day? _____

3. How many lessons is José scheduled for in all? _____

4. Kipley, Naomi, and Mark practice together. Of these students, who is new?
   _____

5. How many new students are there altogether? _____

6. Why does Solina not have a lesson on day 1? _____
   _____

If you could be any animal, which animal would you be? Why?
_____
_____
_____

DAY 9

Geometry/Parts of Speech

Does the dotted line in each figure represent a line of symmetry? Circle *yes* or *no*.

7. yes   no

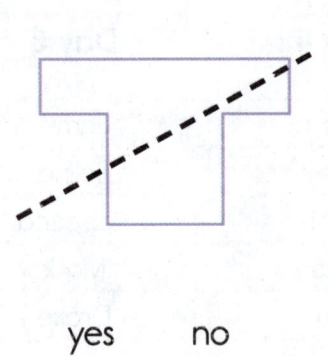

8. yes   no

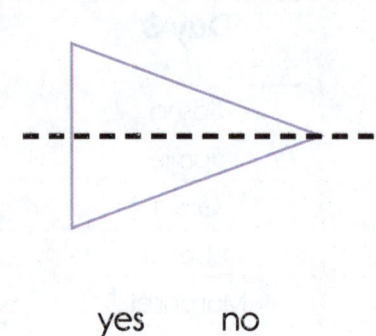

9. yes   no

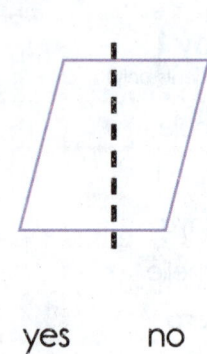

10. yes   no

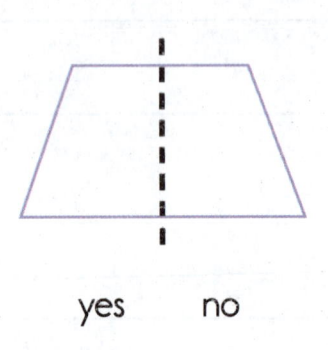

11. yes   no

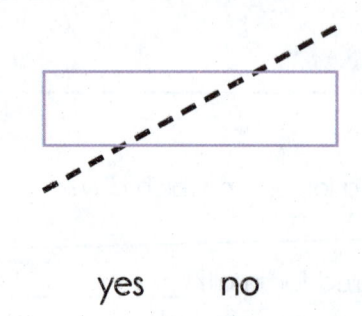

12. yes   no

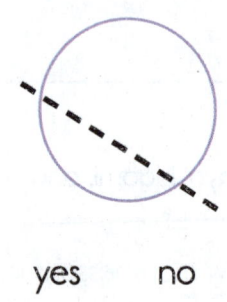

Use the progressive verb tense (a form of *be* + main verb + *ing*) to answer each question.

13. What will you be doing at noon tomorrow?

    I will be eating lunch.

14. What are you working on right now?

    _____

15. What were you doing at this time yesterday?

    _____

16. What will you eat for dinner tomorrow?

    _____

Reading Comprehension

King Midas

One day, King Midas was strolling through his garden. He came across the teacher Silenus, who had taken ill. Midas nursed the old man back to health. The Greek god Dionysus was joyful at the return of his beloved friend Silenus. He allowed the king to make one wish, though he warned him to choose wisely.

King Midas decided quickly. "I would like to have everything I touch turn to gold," he said. Dionysus found the king to be very foolish. Still, he granted the wish.

King Midas grabbed a twig from a tree. His fingers touched the branch, and it immediately turned to gold. Amazing! thought the king. Once he returned home, he ran from room to room, turning things to gold. A golden chair! Golden flowers! A golden staircase!

When the king sat down to feast that night, he reached for a loaf of bread. It turned to gold in his hands. He tried to spoon vegetables onto his plate and sip from his cup of water, but they, too, turned to gold. The king's daughter entered the room at that moment. She saw the look of worry on her father's face and rushed to hug him. He did not have time to warn her away, and the beautiful young girl turned into a statue of gold.

1. Why does Dionysus offer to grant a wish for the king? _____

    _____

2. Why does Dionysus find the king to be foolish? _____

    _____

3. What lesson does this myth teach? What other genre of writing often has a moral or lesson?

    _____

4. What do you think will happen next in the story? _____

    _____

DAY 10 — Fractions/Writing

Skill IDs: 9RJ • KWL

Add to find each sum. Before adding, you may need to change the denominator of one fraction from 10 to 100. Remember to multiply both the numerator and denominator by 10.

5. $\frac{3}{10} + \frac{4}{100} = $ _____

6. $\frac{50}{100} + \frac{2}{10} = $ _____

7. $\frac{7}{10} + \frac{12}{100} = $ _____

8. $\frac{15}{100} + \frac{5}{10} = $ _____

9. $\frac{1}{10} + \frac{85}{100} = $ _____

10. $\frac{66}{100} + \frac{4}{100} = $ _____

11. $\frac{9}{10} + \frac{5}{100} = $ _____

12. $\frac{3}{10} + \frac{60}{100} = $ _____

13. $\frac{49}{100} + \frac{4}{10} = $ _____

14. $\frac{4}{10} + \frac{16}{100} = $ _____

Write about your experience of learning how to do something new. Who helped you? What did you learn? Share your story using a logical sequence of events.

_____

_____

_____

_____

_____

Fast Fun Fact

The oldest surviving fictional story was written almost 4,000 years ago. It's called *The Epic of Gilgamesh*.

Language Arts

Look at each underlined idiom. Then, choose the correct meaning of each sentence.

1. Cody was <u>back to square one</u> when his dog chewed his science fair project.
   A. Cody stood on a square that was labeled *one*.
   B. Cody had to start his science fair project again from the beginning.
   C. Cody was unhappy that his dog chewed up his science fair project.

2. <u>Time flies</u> when we are having fun.
   A. Time seems to go quickly when we are having fun.
   B. Time has wings and flies like a bird.
   C. Time goes slowly.

3. Torika needs to <u>toe the line</u> if she wants to go to the movies.
   A. Torika needs to behave if she wants to go to the movies.
   B. Torika needs to stand behind a line if she wants to go to the movies.
   C. Torika needs to stand in line for a movie ticket.

4. "I liked the book so much that the report is going to be <u>a piece of cake</u>," said Omar.
   A. Omar liked his book, so he thinks the report will be sweet.
   B. Omar liked his book and is going to eat a piece of cake.
   C. Omar liked his book, so he thinks the report will be easy.

5. Nadia was feeling <u>under the weather</u>, so she stayed home from school.
   A. Nadia stayed home from school because the weather was bad.
   B. Nadia stayed home from school because she was sick.
   C. Nadia stayed home from school because she was feeling scared.

Mindful Moment

What is one thing you can do now that you couldn't do in second grade? On a separate sheet of paper, write a letter to yourself to let second-grade you know what you accomplished.

DAY 11

Subtraction/Writing

Subtract to find each difference. Regroup if needed.

6. $7.36
   − $3.97

7. $8.90
   − $2.49

8. $3.85
   − $2.79

9. $7.47
   − $4.58

10. $4.76
    − $2.67

11. $6.89
    − $4.78

12. $6.77
    − $2.88

13. $3.76
    − $1.87

What is the best thing you did this summer?

_____

_____

_____

_____

_____

_____

_____

_____

Division/Writing

Solve the problems. Write remainders like this: r4.

1. 3)5,422   2. 8)687   3. 9)1,599   4. 4)428

5. 3)755   6. 4)4,624   7. 7)878   8. 2)2,542

9. 9)374   10. 6)954   11. 9)1,000   12. 3)752

Imagine that you are asked to invent a new word. What would the word be, and what would it mean?

_____

_____

_____

_____

Matter

All matter on Earth exists in one of three states: solid, liquid, or gas. Solids, such as boxes or books, have certain shapes that are difficult to change. Liquids, such as lemonade or orange juice, take the shape of the containers they are in. Gases, such as helium or the air you breathe, spread out to fill the space they are in. It is easy to change water from one state to another. The water you drink is a liquid. When water is heated, as in a pot on the stove, it becomes a gas. This gas is known as steam, or vapor. Steam can be used in a large machine to make electricity. When water is frozen, as in a tray in the freezer, it turns to ice. Ice can be used to help a hurt part of the body heal.

13. What is the main idea of this passage?

   A. Steam is heated water.

   B. All matter exists as a solid, a liquid, or a gas.

   C. Ice cubes make water taste better.

14. What are two examples of solids? _____

15. What are two examples of liquids? _____

16. What are two examples of gases? _____

17. Water can exist as a solid, a liquid, or a gas. What is it called in each state?

   _____

18. How are solids, liquids, and gases different from each other?

   _____

   _____

   _____

Fractions/Vocabulary

Skill IDs: PDU • 5GY

DAY 13

Add to find each sum. Write each answer in simplest form.

1. $\frac{1}{4} + \frac{3}{4} =$

2. $\frac{3}{5} + \frac{2}{5} =$

3. $\frac{3}{7} + \frac{2}{7} =$

4. $\frac{2}{4} + \frac{1}{4} =$

5. $\frac{1}{7} + \frac{1}{7} =$

6. $\frac{1}{6} + \frac{4}{6} =$

Write the correct homophone from the word bank to complete each sentence.

| I | eye | you | ewe | wear | where |

7. My friend and _____ ate sandwiches and apples for lunch.

8. The _____ took care of her lamb.

9. Cory got a speck of dust in his _____.

10. Do you know _____ to put the books away?

11. Would _____ please hand me that pencil?

12. Hillary will _____ her blue shoes today.

Let's Play Today *See page 108.

Play fit freeze tag. One player tags everyone until all of the players are "frozen." Frozen players perform an exercise for 10 seconds, such as jumping jacks or running in place. The last person frozen becomes "it."

DAY 13 — Word Study/Writing

Skill ID: TE5 — Search for this skill ID on IXL.com for more practice!

Circle your answer to each question. Then, underline the root.

13. Which word contains a Latin root that means "to see"?

    spectacles　　　　perimeter　　　　automobile

14. Which word contains a Greek root that means "measure"?

    structure　　　　thermometer　　　　hydrogen

15. Which word contains a Latin root that means "water"?

    automatic　　　　zoology　　　　aquarium

16. Which word contains a Latin root that means "foot"?

    pedal　　　　decade　　　　universe

17. Which word contains a Greek root that means "three"?

    quarter　　　　unicycle　　　　triplets

18. Which word contains a Greek root that means "write or draw"?

    century　　　　autograph　　　　stethoscope

Describe your dream vacation. Where would you go? What would you do?

_____

_____

_____

_____

Reading Comprehension

Health and Fitness

Health and fitness are important for you and your family. If you start good health habits now, you will have a better chance of being a healthy adult later. You may go to physical education class several times a week, but you should also try to stay fit outside of school. You and your family can make healthy choices together. You can choose fresh fruit for dessert instead of cake. Offer to help make dinner one night, and surprise your family by preparing a delicious salad. You can go for a walk together after dinner instead of watching TV. Exercising can help wake up your brain so that you can do a good job on your homework. Making healthy choices may seem hard now, but it will feel good after a while.

1. What is the main idea of this passage?

    A. Going to physical education class is fun.

    B. Making healthy choices is too hard.

    C. Health and fitness are important for you and your family.

2. What might happen if you start good health habits now? _____
_____

3. How does the author support the idea that good health is important? _____
_____

4. What is a better choice than cake for dessert? _____

5. What can you do instead of watching TV after dinner? _____
_____

6. Find another source of information about health and fitness. You can go online with an adult's help or look for a book at the library. On a separate sheet of paper, write a paragraph that summarizes what you have learned about health and fitness.

DAY 14

Fractions/Capitalization

Solve each word problem. Show your work.

7. Isaiah had 2 hours of free time. He spent $\frac{1}{4}$ of an hour eating a snack, $\frac{1}{4}$ of an hour talking with his brother, and $1\frac{1}{4}$ hours reading. How much time did he have left?

8. A grocery clerk placed $\frac{5}{8}$ pound of butter, $\frac{1}{8}$ pound of raisins, $\frac{3}{8}$ pound of lettuce, and 2 pounds of potatoes into a bag. What was the total weight of the items?

Circle each word that needs a capital letter.

4407 ninth street
hillside, maine 04024

march 10, 2024

skateboards and more
6243 rock avenue
detroit, michigan 48201

To whom it may concern:

I am returning my skateboard for repair. it is still under warranty. please repair it and return the skateboard to the address above as soon as possible.

sincerely,

wesley diaz

---

skateboards and more

6243 rock avenue

detroit, michigan 48201

Multiplication/Sentence Structure

Solve the problems.

1. 5,422 × 3
2. 9,260 × 5
3. 285 × 4
4. 3,164 × 8

5. 907 × 6
6. 8,616 × 7
7. 6,182 × 9
8. 5,481 × 2

Separate each run-on sentence into two sentences. Use correct capitalization and punctuation to write the new sentences.

9. Raven has a new backpack it is green and has many zippers.

   _____

10. Katie borrowed my pencil she plans to draw a map.

    _____

11. Zoe is outside she is on the swings.

    _____

12. Zack is helping Dad Elroy is helping Dad too.

    _____

Read the poem. Then, answer the questions.

"Snow-Flakes"
by Mary Mapes Dodge

Whenever a snow-flake leaves the sky,
It turns and turns to say "Good-bye!
Good-bye, dear cloud, so cool and gray!"
Then lightly travels on its way.

And when a snow-flake finds a tree,
"Good-day!" it says—"Good-day to thee!
Thou art so bare and lonely, dear,
I'll rest, and call my comrades here."

But when a snow-flake, brave and meek,
Lights on a rosy maiden's cheek,
It starts—"How warm and soft the day!
'Tis summer!"—and it melts away.

13. Which pattern describes the poem's rhyme scheme?
    A. ABC ABC
    B. AA BB
    C. AB AB

14. What does the author personify in this poem? _____

15. What are the different sections of a poem called?
    A. paragraphs
    B. rhythms
    C. stanzas

16. According to the poem, when does the snowflake think it's summer? _____

Fast Fun Fact

The largest snowflake ever recorded was 15 inches (38 centimeters) in diameter.

Reading Comprehension/Writing

Read the story. Then, answer the questions.

Ames and Ari closed their eyes to shut out the sun's glare. As they sat on the ground, the hot July sun felt good. They could hear the wind blowing softly through the pine trees, making a kind of whispering, murmuring sound. They could hear the creek nearby making soothing, babbling sounds. They could even hear the distant screech of a hawk flying high overhead.

1. Where do you think Ames and Ari are? _____

2. What season of the year is it? _____

3. What could Ames and Ari hear? _____
   _____

4. What would you like to do if you were there? _____
   _____

Imagine that you are having a party to celebrate something good. Write about what you are celebrating. Then, on a separate sheet of paper, design an invitation for your party.

_____
_____
_____
_____
_____
_____

DAY 16

Addition/Place Value

Add to find each sum. Regroup if needed.

5. 246
   +129

6. 500
   +806

7. 924
   +289

8. 1,284
   +2,629

9. 7,762
   +1,473

10. 3,383
    +5,007

11. 4,290
    +2,968

12. 9,542
    + 695

Use the place value chart to write each number or number word.

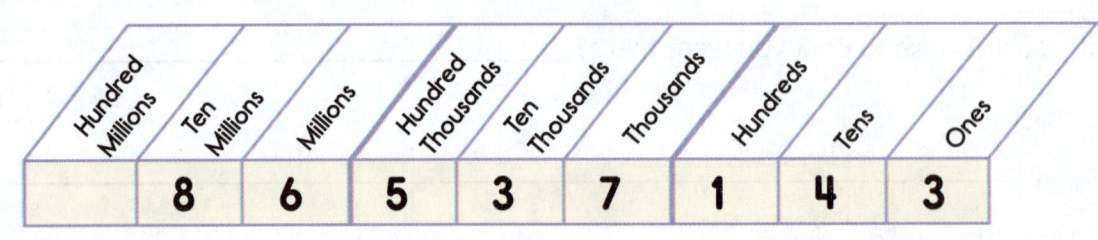

Hundred Millions	Ten Millions	Millions	Hundred Thousands	Ten Thousands	Thousands	Hundreds	Tens	Ones
	8	6	5	3	7	1	4	3

13. Eighty-six million five hundred thirty-seven thousand one hundred forty-three

    86,537,143

14. Five hundred two million one hundred thousand seven _____

15. 375,403,101 _____

Mindful Moment

What is something that made you smile today? Write it down on a separate sheet of paper.

Subtraction/Reading Comprehension

Skill IDs: YDK · XZF

DAY 17

Subtract to find each difference. Regroup if needed.

1. 3.01 − 2.42

2. 5.41 − 3.77

3. 4.71 − 3.82

4. 7.27 − 4.19

5. 5.02 − 3.21

6. 7.04 − 6.67

7. 8.46 − 4.57

8. 6.03 − 2.77

Read the story. Then, answer the questions.

Swimming Lessons

Ann and her brother took swimming lessons this summer. Because they live in the country, they took a bus to the pool. It took half an hour to get there. Their lessons were two hours long, and then they rode the bus home. Even though it took a lot of time, they enjoyed it very much. By the end of the summer, they both knew how to swim well.

9. What is the best summary for this story?

   A. Ann and her brother took swimming lessons this summer.

   B. Ann and her brother rode a bus to the pool to take swimming lessons this summer. They enjoyed it and both learned how to swim.

10. Should a summary be longer or shorter than the original story? _____

11. What information should be included in the summary? _____

_____

_____

_____

© Carson Dellosa Education

141

Rewrite each fraction as a decimal.

12. $\frac{15}{100}$ = _____

13. $\frac{7}{10}$ = _____

14. $\frac{9}{100}$ = _____

15. $\frac{6}{10}$ = _____

16. $\frac{81}{100}$ = _____

17. $\frac{5}{100}$ = _____

18. $\frac{5}{10}$ = _____

19. $\frac{3}{10}$ = _____

Read each group of words. Write S if it is a sentence, F if it is a fragment, or R if it is a run-on sentence.

20. _____ Orangutans are rare animals.

21. _____ Live in rain forests in Borneo and Sumatra.

22. _____ They belong to the ape family along with the chimpanzees and gorillas they are larger than most chimpanzees and smaller than most gorillas.

23. _____ Approximately three to five feet tall.

24. _____ Their arms are extremely long.

Language Arts/Punctuation

| globe | dictionary | encyclopedia |

Where would you find the answer to each of the following questions? Write the name of the best reference from the word bank.

1. Where is Oregon? _____

2. How do they harvest sugarcane in Hawaii? _____

3. Which syllable is stressed in the word *Utah*? _____

4. What kind of food do people eat in Mexico City? _____

5. Which continent is closest to Australia? _____

6. Where is the Indian Ocean? _____

7. Who was Thomas Edison, and what did he do? _____

8. What does the word *hibernate* mean? _____

The proofreading mark ^ is used to show where a word, letter, or punctuation mark needs to be added in a sentence. Use the proofreading mark ⁁ to show where commas are needed in each sentence.

9. As a bird of prey the American kestrel eats insects mice lizards and other birds.

10. Birds of prey such as hawks have hooked beaks and feet with claws.

11. Falcons are powerful fliers and they can swoop from great heights.

12. "Kim let's look at this book about falcons."

Reading Comprehension

Read the passage. Then, answer the questions.

Scientific Experiments

Scientists learn about the world by conducting experiments. They take careful notes about the supplies they use and the results they find. They share their findings with others, which leads to everyone learning a little more. You can do experiments, too! The library has many books with safe experiments for students. You might work with balloons, water, or baking soda. You might learn about how light travels or why marbles roll down a ramp. Ask an adult to help you set up your experiment and make sure that you are being safe. Be sure to wash your hands afterward and clean up the area. Take good notes about your work. Remember, you may be able to change just one thing the next time to get a completely different result. Most of all, do not worry if your results are different from what you expected. Some of the greatest scientific discoveries were made by mistake!

13. What is the main idea of this passage?

   A. Scientists learn about the world by conducting experiments.

   B. Scientists sometimes make mistakes that lead to great discoveries.

   C. You should always take good notes when conducting an experiment.

14. What do scientists take notes about? _____

15. Why should you ask an adult to help you with your experiment? _____

16. Should you worry if you get different results? Why or why not?

_____

Let's Play Today *See page 108.

Run in place for 30 seconds.

Reading Comprehension

Read the story and answer the questions that follow.

Ava, Scientist

Ava had spent every spare moment of the last week working on her science fair project. She aspired to be a scientist one day. It was all she had ever wanted to do. Ava had her mind set on winning first prize. She could think of dozens of ways to use a new, powerful microscope. Her project wasn't going the way she had planned it, though. She pulled the lever, and several metal cans toppled to the floor. Ava stomped her foot with **exasperation**.

"Ava?" said Dad, tapping at her door. "How's it coming? Do you need any help?"

Ava sighed. "Nope, I just have to keep working until I get it right."

1. How would you describe Ava's character? Use details from the story to support your answer.

   _____

   _____

2. What does *exasperation* mean? What clues in the story helped you determine the meaning?

   _____

3. Write a brief summary of the story. _____

   _____

4. Rewrite part of the story using first-person point of view. Be sure to include details that might not be obvious from the third-person point of view.

   _____

   _____

   _____

   _____

Look at the examples of parallel and perpendicular lines. Next to each shape, write how many pairs of parallel sides it has. Then, write how many pairs of perpendicular sides it has. (Your answer may sometimes be 0.)

Parallel Lines   Perpendicular Lines

5.
pairs of parallel sides _____
pairs of perpendicular sides _____

6.
pairs of parallel sides _____
pairs of perpendicular sides _____

7.
pairs of parallel sides _____
pairs of perpendicular sides _____

8.
pairs of parallel sides _____
pairs of perpendicular sides _____

9.
pairs of parallel sides _____
pairs of perpendicular sides _____

Read the passage. Then, follow the directions.

In France, there is a dish similar to pancakes called *crepes*. They are made with flour, eggs, and other ingredients. They are usually rolled up with different kinds of food inside. Most often, they are filled with fruit. In Japan, there are savory pancakes called *okonomiyaki*. They are thin pancakes that come with toppings such as cabbage, meat, and seafood.

On another sheet of paper, write a recipe for your favorite type of pancake. Describe what you like to have on top of them.

Subtraction/Place Value

Skill IDs: 83X • UA7

DAY 20

Subtract to find each difference. Regroup if needed.

1. 5,042 − 1,624
2. 4,200 − 1,122
3. 7,106 − 2,410
4. 3,340 − 1,112

5. 9,824 − 1,224
6. 6,831 − 4,560
7. 7,605 − 1,282
8. 8,001 − 2,381

Round each number to the nearest place shown in parentheses ( ).

9. (ten thousand) 54,220 _____

10. (thousand) 3,728 _____

11. (thousand) 8,922 _____

12. (ten thousand) 46,003 _____

13. (hundred) 614 _____

14. (ten thousand) 18,138 _____

15. (hundred thousand) 198,425 _____

16. (ten thousand) 72,311 _____

Fast Fun Fact

There weren't always specific foods people ate for breakfast! Before the 1600s, breakfast looked more like a snack or dinner.

© Carson Dellosa Education

147

Read the passage. Then, answer the questions.

Flags

A flag tells something special about a country or a group. For example, the United States flag has 13 red and white stripes for the country's first 13 colonies. It has 50 white stars on a blue background to represent the current 50 states. The Canadian flag has a red maple leaf on a white background between two bands of red. The maple tree is the national tree of Canada. Canadian provinces and US states also have their own flags. The state flag of Texas has a large white star on a blue background on the left and two bands of red and white on the right. The star symbolizes Texas's independence from Mexico. Because of the flag's single star, Texas is called the Lone Star State. The flag of the Canadian province New Brunswick has a gold lion on a red background above a sailing ship. The lion stands for ties to Brunswick, Germany, and to the British king. The ship represents the shipping industry.

17. What is the main idea of this passage?

   A. A flag tells something special about the country or group it represents.

   B. Some flags have maple leaves or lions on them.

   C. Many flags are red, white, or blue.

18. What does the United States flag look like? _____

   _____

   _____

19. What does the Canadian flag look like? _____

   _____

   _____

20. Why is Texas called the Lone Star State? _____

   _____

   _____

Science Experiment

Spoon Bell

How can the pitch of sound be changed?

Pitch is a property of sound. A sound's pitch is determined by the frequency of the waves that produce it. Pitch is often described in terms of the highness or lowness of a sound.

Materials:
- 30 inches (76 centimeters) of string
- metal spoon
- table

Procedure:

Tie the handle of the spoon to the center of the string. Wrap the ends of the string around your index fingers.

Place the tip of each index finger in each ear. Lean over so that the spoon hangs freely. Swing the spoon into the side of a table. Listen carefully. Then, record your observations in the chart below.

Shorten the string by wrapping more of it around your fingers. Tap the spoon against the table again. Then, record your observations in the chart below.

Trial	Observations
1	
2	

Which trial was louder? _____

What's This All About?

The vibrating molecules in the spoon hit the string's molecules. The energy is transferred up the string to your ears. When the vibrations travel across a long string, they spread out and have a lower frequency and a lower pitch. When you shorten the string, the movements are more compressed. This results in a higher frequency and a higher pitch.

BONUS — IXL Skill ID 5M4 — Search for this skill ID on IXL.com for more practice!

Science Experiment

Germination

What conditions affect seeds as they germinate?

Materials:

- 2 small, empty jars
- masking tape
- pencil
- scissors
- 10 radish seeds
- sheet of paper towel
- permanent marker
- water

Procedure:

Open one jar. Draw four circles on the paper towel, using the mouth of the jar as your guide. Cut out the circles.

Put one paper towel circle in the bottom of each jar. Then, put five radish seeds on the paper towel circles. Put another paper towel circle over the radish seeds in each jar. Each jar should now have a "sandwich" made of two paper towel circles and five radish seeds.

Add enough water to each jar to moisten, but not drown, the paper towel circles. If you add too much water, pour it out; the seeds will be OK. Label your jars with the pencil and the masking tape. Label one jar *warm* and the other *cold*.

Put the cold jar in the refrigerator. Put the warm jar in a warm, dark place where it will not be disturbed, such as a drawer. Check the seeds every day for four days. Record your observations on a separate sheet of paper.

In which location did the seeds germinate faster? Why do you think this is?

_____

_____

What's This All About?

Several factors affect the germination of seeds. Mainly, seeds are affected by the amount of water available and the temperature. A seed waits until ideal weather conditions exist before sprouting. Some seeds must go through a period of dormancy, or sleep, and endure severe cold before they will germinate. You can put those seeds in a freezer for six weeks so that it feels like winter to them. They will then germinate when planted.

© Carson Dellosa Education

Social Studies

Product Map

A product map uses symbols to show which products are produced in certain places. Below is a product map of Wisconsin. Study the map. Then, answer the questions.

Map Key

- beef cattle
- corn
- fish
- dairy cattle
- chicken
- holiday trees
- snap beans
- hay

1. What product does Wisconsin produce the most of? _____

2. Are more chickens or dairy cattle raised in Wisconsin? _____

3. Which three products are produced the least? _____

4. Judging from the map, does Wisconsin produce more livestock or crops?

   _____

5. Why might it be helpful to know where products are produced? _____

   _____

© Carson Dellosa Education

151

BONUS

Social Studies Activity

Making a Map

Use a print or online atlas to make a map of Africa. Draw and label the features in the list. Then, follow the directions.

Atlas Mountains
Congo River
Hoggar Mountains
Lake Chad
Madagascar (Island)

Lake Tanganyika
Lake Victoria
Namib Desert
Nile River

Mediterranean Sea
Red Sea
Sahara Desert
Strait of Gibraltar

1. Color the deserts orange.
2. Draw brown triangles for the mountains.
3. Draw blue lines and circles for the rivers and lakes.
4. Draw a green line on the equator.
5. Draw red circles on the Tropic of Cancer and the Tropic of Capricorn.

© Carson Dellosa Education

Social Studies Activity

BONUS

Hemisphere

The prime meridian (0° longitude) and the meridian (180° longitude) divide Earth into two halves called the Eastern Hemisphere and the Western Hemisphere. Study the map below. Then, circle the correct hemisphere in parentheses to complete each sentence. Use an atlas or a world map if needed to help you identify each continent.

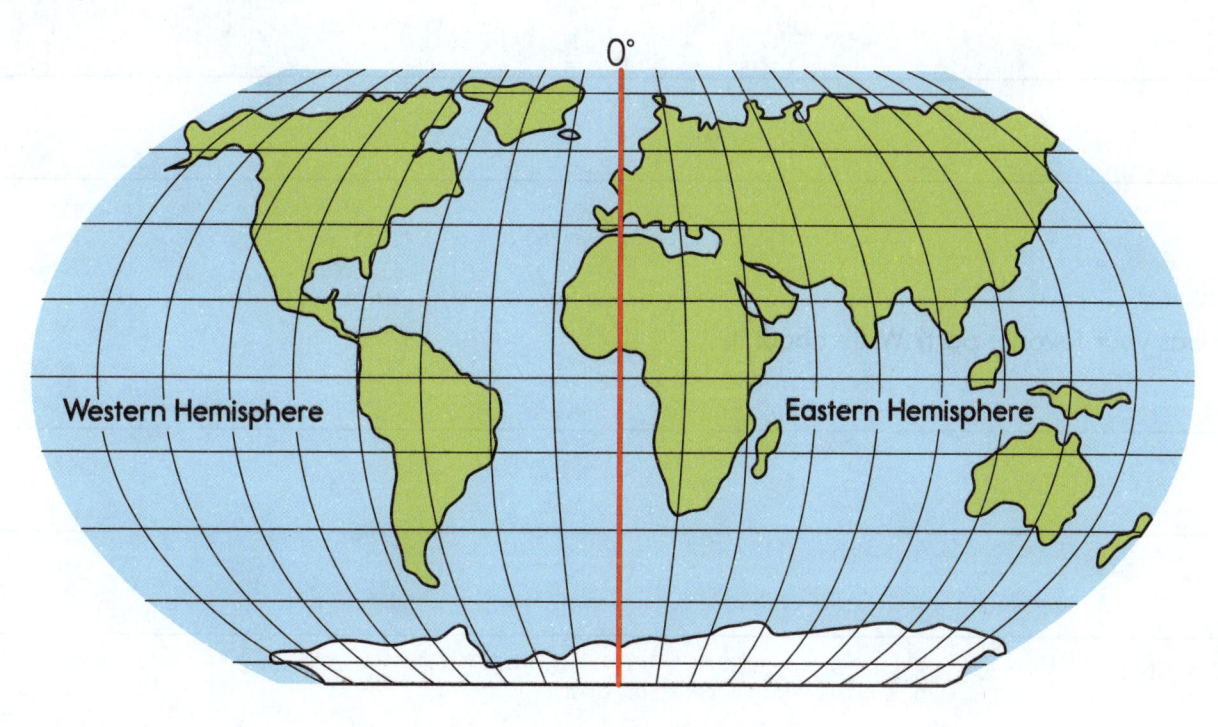

Western Hemisphere   Eastern Hemisphere

1. North America is in the (Eastern, Western) Hemisphere.

2. Asia is mostly in the (Eastern, Western) Hemisphere.

3. Africa is mostly in the (Eastern, Western) Hemisphere.

4. South America is in the (Eastern, Western) Hemisphere.

5. Europe is mostly in the (Eastern, Western) Hemisphere.

6. Australia is in the (Eastern, Western) Hemisphere.

BONUS

Reflect and Reset

Think back on your year of third grade. What was the hardest part? Write about it.

_____

_____

_____

_____

What was your favorite part? Write about it.

_____

_____

_____

_____

What are you most proud of? Write about it.

_____

_____

_____

_____

Reflect and Reset

BONUS

Think ahead to your year of fourth grade. What might be a challenge? Write about it.

_____
_____
_____
_____

What are you looking forward to? Write about it.

_____
_____
_____
_____

Think of three goals that you would like to set for yourself for fourth grade. For example, you may want to join a new club, play a new sport, or improve in math. Write them on the lines.

1. _____

2. _____

3. _____

Answer Key

Section 1

Day 1/Page 13:
1. 324 apples; 2. 5 students; 3. $7.95; 4. $25.25; 5.–10. Answers will vary.; 11. B; 12. when snow hardens into ice over a long period of time; 13. A; 14. Antarctica and Greenland; 15. a lot of snow in winter and cool summers

Day 2/Page 15:
1. play; 2. interest; 3. write; 4. cover; 5. spoon; 6. quick; 7. happy; 8. doubt; 9.–12.

b	r	q	e	o	S	c	r	y	10	6	X
U	y	10	X	2	4	M	z	X	q	a	i
6	v	0	X	8	M	p	2	10	X	12	l
r	b	14	18	b	e	16	f	h	X	E	s
18	X	14	X	2	p	m	n	z	58	20	s
94	86	22	2	R	X	I	0	24	n	x	c
26	39	X	a	d	e	28	g	S	52	X	30
X	j	F	k	32	y	34	4	X	t	10	36
0	n	e	n	38	o	80	98	U	X	x	p
w	m	m	X	N	X	14	31	c	r	e	t
q	u	v	X	X	6	w	X	40	w	X	X

13. SUMMER IS FUN; 14. 3 × 6 = 18; 6 × 3 = 18; 18 ÷ 6 = 3; 18 ÷ 3 = 6; 15. 9 × 4 = 36; 4 × 9 = 36; 36 ÷ 9 = 4; 36 ÷ 4 = 9; 16. 6 × 8 = 48, 8 × 6 = 48, 48 ÷ 6 = 8, 48 ÷ 8 = 6; 17. Crazy, Summer; 18. Let, It; 19. Into; 20. Piney, Woods; 21. How, Train, Your, Dragon; 22. Life, Doesn't, Frighten, Me; 23. Frozen

Day 3/Page 17:
1. 702; 2. 176; 3. 933; 4. 831; 5. 590; 6. 580; 7. 401; 8. 702; 9. Margot's mitten; 10. Salim's bike; 11. birds' chirping; 12. Mariko's goggles; 13. dis-; 14. re-; 15. un- or dis-; 16. un-; 17. in-; 18. in-; 19. dis-; 20. dis- or un-; Answers will vary.; 21. 270; 22. 250; 23. 240; 24. 630

Day 4/Page 19:
1. 18 books; 2. 40 photos; 3. 42 birds; 4. 4 mini muffins; 5. are; 6. make; 7. her; 8. brings; 9. their; 10. try; 11. 750 more tires; 12. 2,250 tires; 13. large; 14. dried; 15. four; 16. good; 17. six; 18. many

Day 5/Page 21:
1. B; 2. 776 BCE, Greece; 3. The International Olympic Committee decided that the summer and winter Olympic Games should be held in different years.; 4. standing for or being an example of; 5. Host countries get a chance to show their culture to athletes, visitors, and spectators.; 6. 12; 7. 16; 8. 2; 9. 14; 10. 9; 11. 20; 13. softer, softest; 14. larger, largest; 15. flatter, flattest; 16. sweeter, sweetest

Day 6/Page 23:
1. 48; 2. 99; 3. 66; 4. 54; 5. 30; 6. 18; 7. 30; 8. 49; 9. 72; 10. 11; 11. 5; 12. 7 13. 2; 14. 6; 15. 6; 16. 9; 17. 11; 18. 8; 19. 32 cups; 20. $1,800; 21. 20 pounds; 22. 435 containers; The following words should be circled: elephant, tent, Mr. Chip, team, book, California, guitar, Lake Street; The following words should be underlined: sang, ate, fixed, laugh, landed, cleaned, yell, played

Day 7/Page 25:
1. respect; 2. satisfaction; 3. silliness; 4. courage; 5. 30 students; 6. There are 95 students in third grade. There are 100 students in fourth grade.; 7. social studies and math; 8. 20 more students like math better than reading in third grade. 25 more students like math better than reading in fourth grade.; 9. 30 10. 90; 11. 10; 12. 40; 13. 800; 14. 800; 15. 200; 16. 600; 17. CX, Before; 18. S; 19. CX, Unless; 20. C, and, but; 21. C, or; 22. CX, Although; 23. C, and; 24. CX, Because

Day 8/Page 27:

1. "I'd like to ride the Ferris wheel first," said Anya.; 2. "The fair seems even more crowded this year than last," commented Riley.; 3. "I can't go on anything that spins," said Kahlil, "because it makes me feel sick."; 4. Anya asked, "What time are you meeting your parents?"; 5. "The line is too long for the rocket ship ride," decided Riley.; 6. 5 × 3 = 15; 7. 7 × 4 = 28; 8. A; 9. A; 10. B; 11. 10 kilograms

Day 9/Page 29:
1. 140; 2. 43; 3. Side A = 80, Side B = 80; 4. Side A = 5, Side B = 5; 5. 51 sq. ft.; 6. 96 sq. in.; 7. C; 8. to help rescue her family and help other enslaved people; 9. the network of people who helped enslaved people escape to freedom; 10. helped move enslaved people to freedom; 11. struggle between northern and southern states, mainly about whether people should be enslaved

Day 10/Page 31:
$\frac{3}{6}, \frac{1}{2}, \frac{2}{3}, \frac{4}{6}, \frac{3}{3}, 1, \frac{1}{4}, \frac{2}{8}$; 2. My dog is ready to play, but my cat wants to nap.; 3. It may rain tonight, so the party will be indoors.; 4. A, B, D; 5. D; 6. A, B, C, D; 7. D; 8. A, B, C, D; 9. D; 10.–11. Sentences will vary.

Day 11/Page 33:
1. numb; 2. knead; 3. certain; 4. purchase; 5. sense; 6. wheat; 7. guide; 8. praise; 9. hour; 10. new; 11. hear; 12. 6; 13. 6; 14. 7; 15. 9; 16. 8; 17. 6; 18. 5; 19. 3; 20.–22. Adjectives will vary.; 23. This or That; 24. This or That; 25. These or Those

Day 12/Page 35:
2. 3; 3. 8; 4. 2; 6. My mom and stepdad were married in Portland, Oregon, on May 1, 1999.; 7. We had sushi, salad, soup, and ice cream for dinner.; 8. George Washington became the first US president on April 30, 1789.; 9. We saw deer, bears, elk, and goats on our trip.; 10. 15, 3 × 5 = 15, 15 ÷ 3 = 5, 15 ÷ 5 = 3; 11. 7, 21 ÷ 7 = 3, 3 × 7 = 21, 7 × 3 = 21; 12. 5, 30 ÷ 5 = 6, 5 × 6 = 30, 6 × 5 = 30; 13. Rocky River, OH 44116;

Answer Key

14. Baltimore, MD 21218; **15.** Harrisburg, PA 17511; **16.** Lincoln, NE 68516; **17.** Portland, OR 97215; **18.** Colton, CA 92324

Day 13/Page 37:

2. 10, 5, 135; **3.** 10, 8, 108; **4.** 6, 6, 240; **5.** 10, 4, 112; **6.** 11, 11, 176; **7.** knock; **8.** hopped; **9.** night; **10.** baby; **11.** different; **12.** A; **13.** Puerto Rico; **14.** Pittsburgh; **15.** helped people in Puerto Rico; **16.** to deliver supplies

Day 14/Page 39:

1. >; **2.** >; **3.** <; **4.** <; **5.** <; **6.** >; **7.** >; **8.** >; **9.** >; **10.** have good luck; **11.** ill; **12.** ability to grow things; **13.** cost a lot; **14.–16.** Answers will vary. Possible answers include:

14. ; **15.** ; **16.** ;

17. 11:20; **18.** 3:47; **19.** 6:04; **20.** 12:40; **21.** 8:55; **22.** 2:28

Day 15/Page 41:

1. 71°, 86 − 9 = 77, 77 − 6 = 71;
2. 1 inch, 4 × 12 = 48, 48 + 4 = 52, 53 − 52 = 1;
3. 6 muffins, 17 + 19 = 36, 42 − 36 = 6;
4. 50 miles, 10:00 to 3:00 = 5 hours, 5 × 10 = 50; **5.** jazz, They are instruments.; **6.** tire, They are tools.; **7.** dog, They are birds.; **8.** Moon, They are planets.; **9.** lazy, They are flowers.;

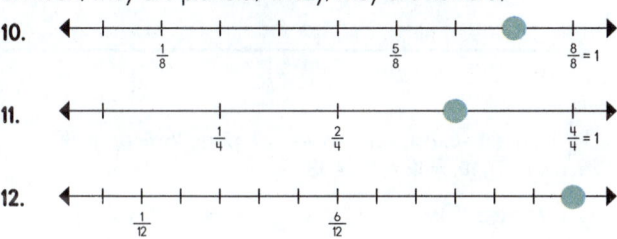

10.

11.

12.

13. will study; **14.** will visit; **15.** will go; **16.** will read; **17.** will show

Day 16/Page 43:

2. action, the state of acting; **3.** safest, most safe, or safety, the state of being safe; **4.** hungriest, most hungry; **5.** preparation, the state of being prepared; **6.** heaviest, most heavy; **7.** I, her; **8.** him; **9.** me; **10.** us; **11.** We; **12.** They; **13.** They, them; **14.** well; **15.** well; **16.** better; **17.** better; **18.** best; **19.** well; **20.** worse; **21.** worse; **22.** better

Day 17/Page 45:

1.–2. Answers will vary.; **4.** -est, sad; **5.** -est, hungry; **6.** -tion, prepare; **7.** -tion, invent; **8.** -ty, taste; **9.** -ty, certain; **10.** -ty, loyal; **11.** -tion, direct; **12.** -est, lovely; **13.** B; **14.** The main character of the Anne of Green Gables series; **15.** She lived with her grandparents and went to school in a one-room schoolhouse.; **16.** when she was 17; **17.** It was a best-seller. Two films and at least seven TV shows have been made from it.; **18.** to see where Anne Shirley grew up

Day 18/Page 47:

1. 80; **2.** 90; **3.** 84; **4.** 96; **5.** 94; **6.** 76; **7.** 76; **8.** 84; **9.** hatched; **10.** looked; **11.** used; **12.** breathed; **13.** changed; **14.** started; **15.** flattened; **16.** vanished; **17.** disappeared; **18.** hopped; **19.–21.** Answers will vary.; **22.** / (slash) or dot; **23.** good;

24. better; **25.** best; **26.** bad; **27.** worst; **28.** good or better

Day 19/Page 49:

1. C; **2.** The ropes sometimes broke.; **3.** pull the elevator back up if the cables broke; **4.** the Eiffel Tower and the Empire State Building; **5.** They continued to sell Otis's design.; **6.** 63; **7.** 24; **8.** 40; **9.** 18; **10.** 15; **11.** 64; **12.** 54; **13.** 21; **14.** 20; **15.** 49; **16.** 48; **17.** 16; Answers will vary.

Day 20/Page 51:

1. 224; **2.** 155; **3.** 190; **4.** 125; **5.** 148; **6.** 207; **7.** 161; **8.** 166; **11.** L; **12.** A; **13.** L; **14.** L; **15.** A; **16.** A; **17.** L; **18.** A; **19.** A; **20.** A; **21.** L; **22.** L; **23.** A; **24.** L; **25.** 42; **26.** 31; **27.** 34; **28.** 31; **29.** 10; **30.** 11; **31.** 23; **32.** 11; **33.** P, F, PR; **34.** PR, F, P; **35.** F, PR, P; **36.** F, P, PR

Bonus Page 53:

1. The water causes the ink to dissolve and travel along the coffee filter.; **2.** The inks separated into different colors.; **3.** Answers will vary.; **4.** able to dissolve in water

Bonus Page 54:

1. The higher the ramp, the faster the object traveled.; **2.** Answers will vary.; **3.** It rolls faster.; **4.** It asks a question that will be answered by doing the experiment.; **5.** It makes it easy for the experimenter to see the relationship between the height of the ramp and the speed of the car.

Bonus Page 55:

1. 0; **2.** W; **3.** E; **4.** Students should trace the prime meridian.

Bonus Page 56:

1. 500 km; **2.** 175 km; **3.** 550 km; **4.** 900 km

Bonus Page 57:

1. E; **2.** H; **3.** F; **4.** J; **5.** C; **6.** D; **7.** G; **8.** I; **9.** B; **10.** A

Section 2
Day 1/Page 61:

1. D; **2.** A; **3.** C; **4.** B; **5.** A; **6.** C; **7.** D; **8.** B; Answers will vary.; **10.** "Where is the big beach ball?" asked Malik.; **11.** Mei exclaimed, "That is a wonderful idea!"; **12.** "Come and do your work," Grandma said, "or you can't go with us."; **13.** "Yesterday," said Ella, "I saw a pretty robin in the tree by my window."; **14.** "I will always take care of my pets," promised Theodore.; **15.** Rachel said, "Maybe we should have practiced more."; **16.** Dr. Jacobs asked, "How are you, Kade?"; Students' writing will vary.

Day 2/Page 63:

Students' writing will vary.; The following words should be written under Common Nouns: ocean, class, holiday, boat, beans.; The following words should be written under Proper Nouns: Monday, November, July, Rex, North Carolina.; **1.** B; **2.** C; **3.** two; **4.** cent; **5.** to; **6.** sent; **7.** too; **8.** scent

Day 3/Page 65:

1. re–, to move again; **2.** un–, not usual; **3.** re–, to make new again; **4.** un–, not common; **5.** re–, to tell again; **7.** umbrella; **8.** Juan; **9.** Amira and Becca; **10.** Nia; **11.** toy; **12.** bus; **13.** warm; **14.** worried; **15.** who; **16.** weigh; **17.** want; **18.** wonderful; **19.** children; **20.** where; **21.** teeth

© Carson Dellosa Education

157

Answer Key

Day 4/Page 67:
1. $\overrightarrow{AB}$; 2. $\overleftrightarrow{GH}$; 3. $\overleftrightarrow{LM}$; 4. $\overleftrightarrow{CD}$; 5. $\overleftrightarrow{UT}$; 6. $\overrightarrow{WX}$; Students' writing will vary.; 7. pears; 8. seem; 9. flour; 10. right; 11. won; 12. dough; 13. B; 14. A; 15. C; 16. C; 17. A

Day 5/Page 69:
1. 3:30; 2. 55 minutes; 3. 6, 6; 4. 3, 3; 5. 8, 8; 6. 4, 4; 7. 4, 4; 8. 4, 4; 9. Shapes in #6, #7, and #8 have the same number of sides and vertices.; 10. 13,011; 11. 1,410; 12. 166; 13. 1,350; 14. 180; 15. 1,305; 16. 24,672; 17. 8,696; 19.–23. Students should circle the words in blue: 19. drive slowly; 20. often begins; 21. cheers excitedly; 22. pass near; 23. decorated beautifully

Day 6/Page 71:
1. 8, 16, 12, 18, 14; 2. 21, 15, 6, 12, 24; 3. 40, 32, 16, 28, 24, 36; 4. 45, 10, 30, 25, 35, 20; 5. pictures; 6. market; 7. cottage; 8. quarter; 9. pennies; 10. circus; 11. bell; 12. curtains; 13. 60; 14. 60; 15. 110; 16. 90; 17. 70; 18. 50; 19. 80; 20. 30; 21. read; 22. knew; 23. told; 24. said; 25. heard; 26. bought; 27. ate; 28. built

Day 7/Page 73:
1. 28, 32, and 18; 2. 16, 22, and 72; 3. 71, 82, and 98; 4. 63, 25, and 61; 5. 100, 206, and 200; 6. 79, 20, and 90; 7. make; 8. rolled; 9. enjoyed; 10. helps or helped; 11. painted; 12. I rode down the hill on a bike.; 13. My mom and I planted a garden in our backyard.; 14. All of the animals braced themselves when the elephants sneezed.; 15. 50; 16. 157; 17. 116; 18. 172

Day 8/Page 75:
1. My family visits Spring Grove, Minnesota, every year in the summer.; 2. Dear Grandpa,; 3. Yours truly,; 4. On October 9, 2009, Carolyn saw the play.; 5. My aunt and uncle live in North Branch, New York.; 6. Dear Jon,; 7. January 1, 2010; 8. Paris, Texas, is located in the northeastern part of the state.; 9. 150 liters; 10. 1 liter; 11. 10 kilograms; 12. 100 grams; 13. 11 inches; 14. 15 centimeters; 15. 92; 16. 30; 17. 33; 18. 125; 19. 51; 20. 64; 21. 16; 22. 71; 23. 18; 24. 40; 25. 22; 26. 17 27. 90 students

Day 9/Page 77:
1. 3; 2. 2; 3. 5; 4. 4; 5. correct; 6. correct; 7. careful; 8. correct; 9. garden; 10. babies; 11. correct; 12. correct; 13. movie; 14. correct; 15. He lets people borrow his skateboard, and he can be counted on.; 16. Yes, because she takes turns and is fair.; 17. Answers will vary but may include going to school, going to summer camp, going to the recreation center, skateboarding, and riding bikes.; 18. It means that someone is always helpful and dependable.

Day 10/Page 79:
1. 36 people; 2. 144 plates; 3. 28 times as old; 4. 128 water balloons; 5.–6. Answers will vary.; 7. 394; 8. 663; 9. 28; 10. 226; 11. 312; 12. 2,688; 13. 3,589; 14. 2,835; 15.–20. Students should circle the words in blue.; 15. The girls were planning a sleepover for Friday.; 16. Samir has read that book at least three times.; 17. Colin has used that same duffel bag for the last five years.; 18. Brandy will bring snacks to the game.; 19. Zara is getting a dog tomorrow; 20. Tonight, we are studying for the quiz at Annie's house.

Day 11/Page 81:
1. 14,485; 2. 17,723; 3. 2,074; 4. 7,658; 5. 1,244; 6. 18,621; 7. 19,739; 8. 15,878; 9. snowflakes, dancers; 10. highway, parking lot; 11. tornado, train; 12. fingers, icicles; 14. 1,847; 15. 4,280; 16. 9,999; 17. positive; 18. magnify; 19. follow; 20. urgent; 21. nurse; 22. twirl; 23. return; 24. worse

Day 12/Page 83:
1. 561, 500 + 60 + 1; 2. 4,826, 4,000 + 800 + 20 + 6; 3. 2,121; 4. 3,211; 5. H; 6. E; 7. B; 8. C; 9. D; 10. A; 11. G; 12. F; 13. give the sunglasses to the girl; 14. Answers will vary.; Last summer, we went camping in Colorado. We went hiking and swimming every day. One time, I actually saw a baby white-tailed deer with spots. We also took photos of a lot of pretty rocks, flowers, and leaves. We had a great time. I didn't want to leave.

Day 13/Page 85:
1. 98°, obtuse; 2. 63°, acute; 3. 70°, 25°, 70° + 25° = 95°; 4. B; 5. Empty the package into a microwave-safe bowl.; 6. water, milk, oatmeal, microwave-safe bowl, spoon, measuring cup; 7. B; 8. <; 9. >; 10. >; 11. <; 12. <; 13. <; 14. >; 15. <; 16. <

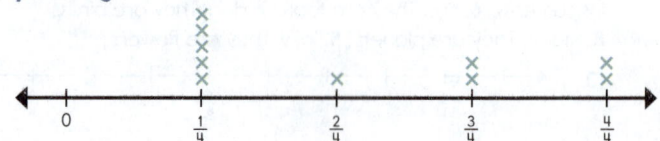

Day 14/Page 87:
$1\frac{1}{4}$ inches; 1.–6. Answers will vary.; 7. page 16; 8. page 40; 9. page 57; 10. ≠; 11. =; 12. ≠; 13. =

Day 15/Page 89:
1. 78 × 9 = 702; 2. 2,542 – 1,268 = 1,274; Students' writing will vary.; 3. B; 4. A; 6.–9. Answers will vary.

Day 16/Page 91:
The following words should have three lines drawn beneath the first letter: Jane Goodall, Hampstead, London, Jubilee, Goodall, Gombe Stream National Park, Cambridge, Jane Goodall, Fifi, David, United Nations Messenger Peace.; 1. Penny's dog Coco likes to eat special snacks.; 2. Oliver Owl is teaching Owen Owl to fly.; Students' writing will vary. 3.-4. Answers will vary.

Day 17/Page 93:
1. cm; 2. m; 3. cm, cm; 4. km; 5. km; 6. m; 7. m; 8. km; 10. >; 11. <; 12. >; 13. >; 14. <; 15. <; 16. <; 17. >; 18. >; 19. =; 20. <; 21. 4 × 5 = 20 books; 22. 133 ÷ 7 = 19 times as many; 23. Brooke will stay and tell Ms. Havel what happened.; 24. Answers will vary.

Answer Key

Day 18/Page 95:
1. $\frac{7}{12}$; **2.** $\frac{7}{8}$; **3.** $\frac{4}{6}$; **4.** $\frac{9}{10}$; **5.** who; **6.** who; **7.** which; **8.** that; **9.–10.** Answers will vary.; **11.** A; **12.** S; **13.** S; **14.** A; **15.** A; **16.** S; **17.** S; **18.** A; **19.** A; **20.** A; **21.** A; **22.** S; Earth, plant, Plants, oxygen, sunlight, heat

Day 19/Page 97:
1. 112; **2.** 112; **3.** 52; **4.** 18; **5.** 55; **6.** 91; **7.** 72; **8.** 168; **9.** 110; **10.** 566; **11.** 54; **12.** 570; **13.** two; **14.** read; **15.** too; **16.** Red; **17.** to; **18.** 1; **19.** $\frac{3}{2}$ or $1\frac{1}{2}$; **20.** $\frac{1}{3}$; **21.** $\frac{2}{5}$; **22.** 1; **23.** 1; **24.** 1; **25.** $\frac{7}{5}$ or $1\frac{2}{5}$; **26.** $\frac{3}{5}$; The following words should be written under *Compound Words*: buttermilk, airplane, snowstorm, football, daylight.; The following words should be written under *Words with Prefixes or Suffixes*: selection, replanted, sleepless, peaceful, unpacked.

Day 20/Page 99:
1. A; **2.** A lot of rain falls quickly and fills the streets faster than they can drain.; **3.** It could be swept away.; **4.** listen to radio or TV news reports; **5.** The author supports the point by stating the facts that trying to drive or walk in high water is very dangerous and that tap water can be made unsafe for drinking.; **6.** $\frac{3}{4}$; **7.** $\frac{5}{3}$ or $1\frac{2}{3}$; **8.** $\frac{12}{12}$ or 1; **9.** $\frac{30}{8}$ or $3\frac{6}{8}$; **10.** picture; **11.** thoughtful; **12.** appointment

Bonus Page 101:
Answers will vary.

Bonus Page 102:
heterogeneous

Bonus Page 103:
1. O; **2.** N; **3.** S; **4.** Students should trace the equator.

Bonus Page 104:
1. Calgary; **2.** Denver; **3.** Boston; **4.** Charleston; **5.** Montreal; **6.** Salt Lake City; **7.** San Francisco

Bonus Page 105:
Drawings will vary.

Section 3
Day 1/Page 109:
1. 312; **2.** 1,617; **3.** 2,436; **4.** 2,142; **5.** 7,332; **6.** 2,592; **7.** 414; **8.** 2,035; **9.** 1,798; **10.** 3,450; **11.** go shopping for new clothes; **12.** Answers will vary.; **14.** $2.50; **15.** $0.05; **16.** $0.20; **17.** $3.58; **18.** $10.65; **19.** $0.45; **20.** $6.05; **21.** $15.00; **22.** deceive; **23.** accompany; **24.** exercise; **25.** sincerely; **26.** particular; **27.** patient; **28.** friend; **29.** because; **30.** guard; **31.** although

Day 2/Page 111:
1. A; **2.** a drawing that shows how different living things are connected; **3.** B; **4.** by explaining how all living things are connected in an ecosystem's food web; **5.** 10; **6.** 24; **7.** 2; **8.** 4; **9.** 2; **10.** 20; **11.** 4; **12.** 12; **13.** 8 cups; **14.** 2 gallons

Day 3/Page 113:
Answers will vary, but students should include support for their opinions.; **2.** O; **3.** O; **4.** F; **5.** O; **6.** F; **7.** F; **8.** F; **9.** O; **10.** O; **11.** A; **12.** newsreels in movie theaters or articles in newspapers; **13.** Answers will vary. Possible answer: Edward Murrow was an American journalist who became famous for reporting from London on the radio during WWII.; **14.** He started interviewing important people.

Day 4/Page 115:
1. 1 × 12, 2 × 6, 3 × 4; **2.** 1 × 15, 3 × 5; **3.** 1 × 36, 2 × 18, 3 × 12, 4 × 9, 6 × 6; **4.** 1 × 24, 2 × 12, 3 × 8, 4 × 6; **5.** 1 × 28, 2 × 14, 4 × 7; **6.** 1 × 32, 2 × 16, 4 × 8; **7.** equal to; **8.** less than; **9.** less than; **10.** more than; **11.** less than; **12.** equal to; **13.** F, I; **14.** I, F; **15.** F, I; **16.** 15, 18, 21, 27; **17.** 30, 36, 42, 54, 60; **18.** 28, 32, 36, 40, 48; **19.** 21, 18, 15, 12, 6; **20.** 92, 90, 88, 84, 82

Day 5/Page 117:
1. read the books about Mexico to her grandmother; **2.** Answers will vary.; **4.** $\frac{3}{10}$ or 0.3; **5.** $\frac{9}{10}$ or 0.9; **6.** $\frac{7}{10}$ or 0.7; **7.** $\frac{1}{10}$ or 0.10; **8.** $\frac{5}{10}$ or 0.5; **9.** 0.3; **10.** 1.7; **11.** 3.5; **12.** $1\frac{9}{10}$; **13.** $\frac{8}{10}$; **14.** $3\frac{4}{10}$; **16.** small pink teacup; **17.** cozy gray wool sweater; **18.** three large yellow plastic trucks; **19.** small fresh Greek salad; **20.** striped venomous snake; **21.** sticky; **22.** four; **23.** helpful; **24.** blue

Day 6/Page 119:
1. group of people living together; **2.** in the city; **3.** in the country; **4.** $\frac{1}{6}$; **5.** $\frac{2}{10}$ or $\frac{1}{5}$; **6.** $\frac{1}{4}$; **7.** $3\frac{4}{10}$ or $3\frac{2}{5}$; **8.** $5\frac{1}{10}$; **9.** $4\frac{1}{15}$; **10.** Answers will vary. Possible answers follow. Elizabeth is a hard worker. She worries about her family and their farm. She is grateful when neighbors help out and hopeful about the future. **11.** Tasks are easier when people work together. **12.** first-person point of view, We learn about what Elizabeth's life is like and what her thoughts are. The reader gets the inside point of view.

Day 7/Page 121:
1. 1,500; **2.** 25; **3.** 1,000; **4.** $\frac{1}{2}$; **5.** 3; **6.** 15; **8.–14.** Students should circle the phrases in yellow.; **8.** <u>The temperature dropped overnight</u>, so frost covered the windows.; **9.** <u>The falling snowflakes</u> made my cheeks wet and cold.; **10.** Snow stuck to my mittens <u>because I had made a snowman</u>.; **11.** The snowman melted <u>from the heat of the sun</u>.; **12.** <u>I swam so long in the pool</u> that I had to put on more sunscreen.; **13.** Cayce missed the bus <u>because she overslept</u>.; **14.** <u>Because Shay watched a scary movie on TV</u>, she could not fall asleep.; Answers will vary, but students should include descriptive details and dialogue in their writing.; **15.** <; **16.** <; **17.** >; **18.** <; **19.** >; **20.** >; **21.** >; **22.** <; **23.** <; **24.** =; **25.** <; **26.** <

Day 8/Page 123:
1. B; **2.** It is easy to get from one point in a city to another.; **3.** A; **4.** after a fire destroyed most of London, England; **5.** Philadelphia's streets are wide, organized, and easy to walk down, and London's streets are not.; **6.–9.** Check students' work for symmetry.; **10.** hard; **11.** honk; **12.** fingers; **13.** round; **14.** fly; **15.** small

© Carson Dellosa Education

Answer Key

Day 9/Page 125:
1. Greg, Kipley, José, and Kira; **2.** Day 1; **3.** 2; **4.** Naomi; **5.** five; **6.** She is not a new student.; Students' writing will vary.; **7.** no; **8.** yes; **9.** no; **10.** yes; **11.** no; **12.** no; **14.–16.** Answers will vary.

Day 10/Page 127:
1. He wants to thank the king for helping Silenus.; **2.** Dionysus is wiser than the king. He realizes that changing everything to gold is a terrible idea.; **3.** Be careful what you wish for, and don't be greedy. Fables also have morals.; **4.** The king will ask Dionysus to reverse his wish.; **5.** $\frac{34}{100}$; **6.** $\frac{70}{100}$; **7.** $\frac{82}{100}$; **8.** $\frac{65}{100}$; **9.** $\frac{95}{100}$; **10.** $\frac{70}{100}$; **11.** $\frac{95}{100}$; **12.** $\frac{90}{100}$; **13.** $\frac{89}{100}$; **14.** $\frac{56}{100}$; Answers will vary, but students' writing should include a logical sequence of events.

Day 11/Page 129:
1. B; **2.** A; **3.** A; **4.** C; **5.** B; **6.** $3.39; **7.** $6.41; **8.** $1.06; **9.** $2.89; **10.** $2.09; **11.** $2.11; **12.** $3.89; **13.** $1.89; Students' writing will vary.

Day 12/Page 131:
1. 1,807 r1; **2.** 85 r7; **3.** 177 r6; **4.** 107; **5.** 251 r2; **6.** 1,156; **7.** 125 r3; **8.** 1,271; **9.** 41 r5; **10.** 159; **11.** 111 r1; **12.** 250 r2; Students' writing will vary.; **13.** B; **14.** Answers will vary but may include: boxes and books.; **15.** Answers will vary but may include: lemonade and orange juice.; **16.** Answers will vary but may include: air and helium.; **17.** ice, water, steam/vapor; **18.** Solids have a certain shape that is difficult to change. Liquids take the shape of the container they are in. Gases fill the space they are in.

Day 13/Page 133:
1. 1; **2.** 1; **3.** $\frac{5}{7}$; **4.** $\frac{3}{4}$; **5.** $\frac{2}{7}$; **6.** $\frac{5}{6}$; **7.** I; **8.** ewe; **9.** eye; **10.** where; **11.** you; **12.** wear; **13.** spectacles; **14.** thermometer; **15.** aquarium; **16.** pedal; **17.** triplets; **18.** autograph; Students' writing will vary.

Day 14/Page 135:
1. C; **2.** You will have a better chance of being a healthy adult later.; **3.** The author gives the reasons that good health now can help you with your homework and help you become a healthy adult later.; **4.** fresh fruit; **5.** go for a walk with your family; **6.** Students' paragraphs will vary.; **7.** $\frac{1}{4} + \frac{1}{4} + 1\frac{1}{4} = 1\frac{3}{4}$, $2 - 1\frac{3}{4} = \frac{1}{4}$ hour; **8.** $\frac{5}{8} + \frac{1}{8} + \frac{3}{8} + 2 = 2\frac{9}{8} = 3\frac{1}{8}$ pounds; The following words should be circled: Ninth, Street, Hillside, Maine, March, Skateboards, More, Rock, Avenue, Detroit, Michigan, Whom, It, May, Concern, It, Please, Sincerely, Wesley, Diaz, Skateboards, More, Rock, Avenue, Detroit, Michigan.

Day 15/Page 137:
1. 16,266; **2.** 46,300; **3.** 1,140; **4.** 25,312; **5.** 5,442; **6.** 60,312; **7.** 55,638; **8.** 10,962; **9.** Raven has a new backpack. It is green with many zippers.; **10.** Katie borrowed my pencil. She plans to draw a map.; **11.** Zoe is outside. She is on the swings.; **12.** Zack is helping Dad. Elroy is helping Dad too.; **13.** B; **14.** snowflakes; **15.** C; **16.** when it lands on a rosy maiden's cheek

Day 16/Page 139:
1. Answers will vary but may include: a forest, in the woods.; **2.** summer; **3.** the wind blowing through the pine trees, the creek nearby, and the screech of a hawk; **4.** Answers will vary.; Students' writing will vary.; **5.** 375; **6.** 1,306; **7.** 1,213; **8.** 3,913; **9.** 9,235; **10.** 8,390; **11.** 7,258; **12.** 10,237; **14.** 502,100,007; **15.** three hundred seventy-five million four hundred three thousand one hundred one

Day 17/Page 141:
1. 0.59; **2.** 1.64; **3.** 0.89; **4.** 3.08; **5.** 1.81; **6.** 0.37; **7.** 3.89; **8.** 3.26; **9.** B; **10.** shorter; **11.** Answers will vary but may include: key points, main idea, names of characters.; **12.** 0.15; **13.** 0.7; **14.** 0.09; **15.** 0.6; **16.** 0.81; **17.** 0.05; **18.** 0.5; **19.** 0.3; **20.** S; **21.** F; **22.** R; **23.** F; **24.** S

Day 18/Page 143:
1. globe; **2.** encyclopedia; **3.** dictionary; **4.** encyclopedia; **5.** globe; **6.** globe; **7.** encyclopedia; **8.** dictionary; **9.** As a bird of prey, the American kestrel eats insects, mice, lizards, and other birds.; **10.** Birds of prey, such as hawks, have hooked beaks and feet with claws.; **11.** Falcons are powerful fliers, and they can swoop from great heights.; **12.** "Kim, let's look at this book about falcons."; **13.** A; **14.** the supplies they use and the results they find; **15.** to help you set up and make sure you are being safe; **16.** No, because some of the greatest scientific discoveries were made by mistake.

Day 19/Page 145:
1.–4. Answers will vary. Possible answers shown. **1.** Ava is intelligent, persistent, and a little stubborn. She is very interested in science and she doesn't give up. She won't accept help.; **2.** frustration, annoyance; Her project isn't going as planned, and she stomps her foot.; **3.** Ava, who hopes to be a scientist one day, is working on a science fair project. She has some trouble but keeps working at it.; **4.** Answers will vary.; **5.** 2, 4; **6.** 0, 1; **7.** 2, 0; **8.** 1, 0; **9.** 3, 2; Students' writing will vary.

Day 20/Page 147:
1. 3,418; **2.** 3,078; **3.** 4,696; **4.** 2,228; **5.** 8,600; **6.** 2,271; **7.** 6,323; **8.** 5,620; **9.** 50,000; **10.** 4,000; **11.** 9,000; **12.** 50,000; **13.** 600; **14.** 20,000; **15.** 200,000; **16.** 70,000; **17.** A; **18.** It has 13 red and white stripes and 50 white stars on a blue field.; **19.** It has a red maple leaf on a white background between two bands of red.; **20.** There is a single star on the state flag that symbolizes Texas's independence from Mexico.

Bonus Page 149:
The second trial was louder.

Bonus Page 150:
the warm jar; Answers will vary.

Bonus Page 151:
1. dairy cattle; **2.** dairy cattle; **3.** fish, chicken, and beef cattle; **4.** crops; **5.** Answers will vary.

Bonus Page 152:
Check students' drawings against an atlas for accuracy.

Bonus Page 153:
1. Western; **2.** Eastern; **3.** Eastern; **4.** Western; **5.** Eastern; **6.** Eastern

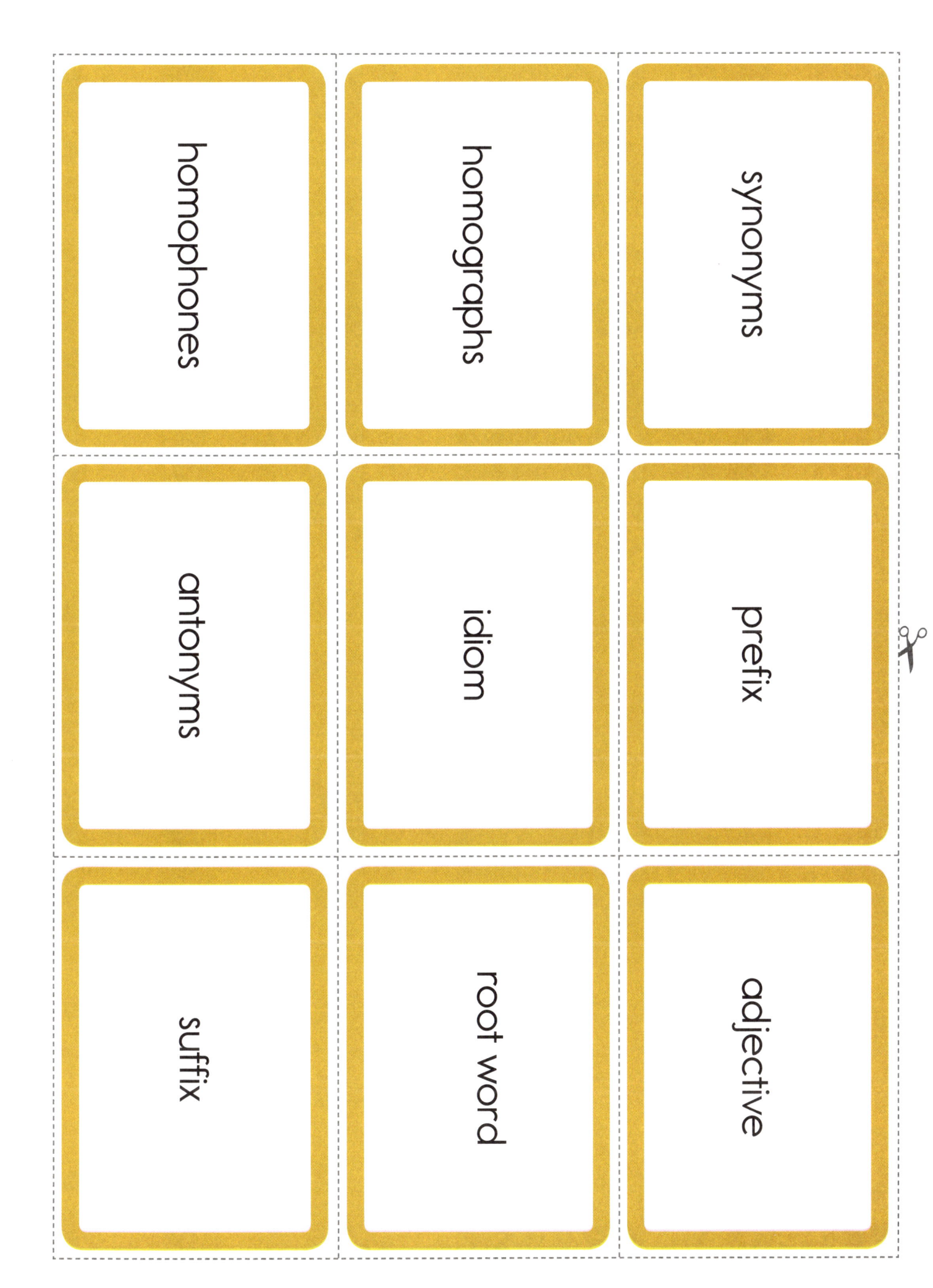

homophones	homographs	synonyms
antonyms	idiom	prefix
suffix	root word	adjective

words that have the same or nearly the same meaning **happy, joyful**	words that are spelled the same but have different meanings **bat (animal), bat (baseball)**	words that sound the same but have different spellings and meanings **to, too, two**
a word part added to the beginning of a word to change its meaning **un-, re-, dis-**	a common expression whose meaning is not obvious **Break a leg!**	words that have opposite meanings **hot, cold**
a word that describes a noun or pronoun **blue, small, cute**	a word a prefix or suffix is added to **happy (unhappy, happiness)**	a word part added to the end of a word to change its meaning **-ness, -ment, -er**

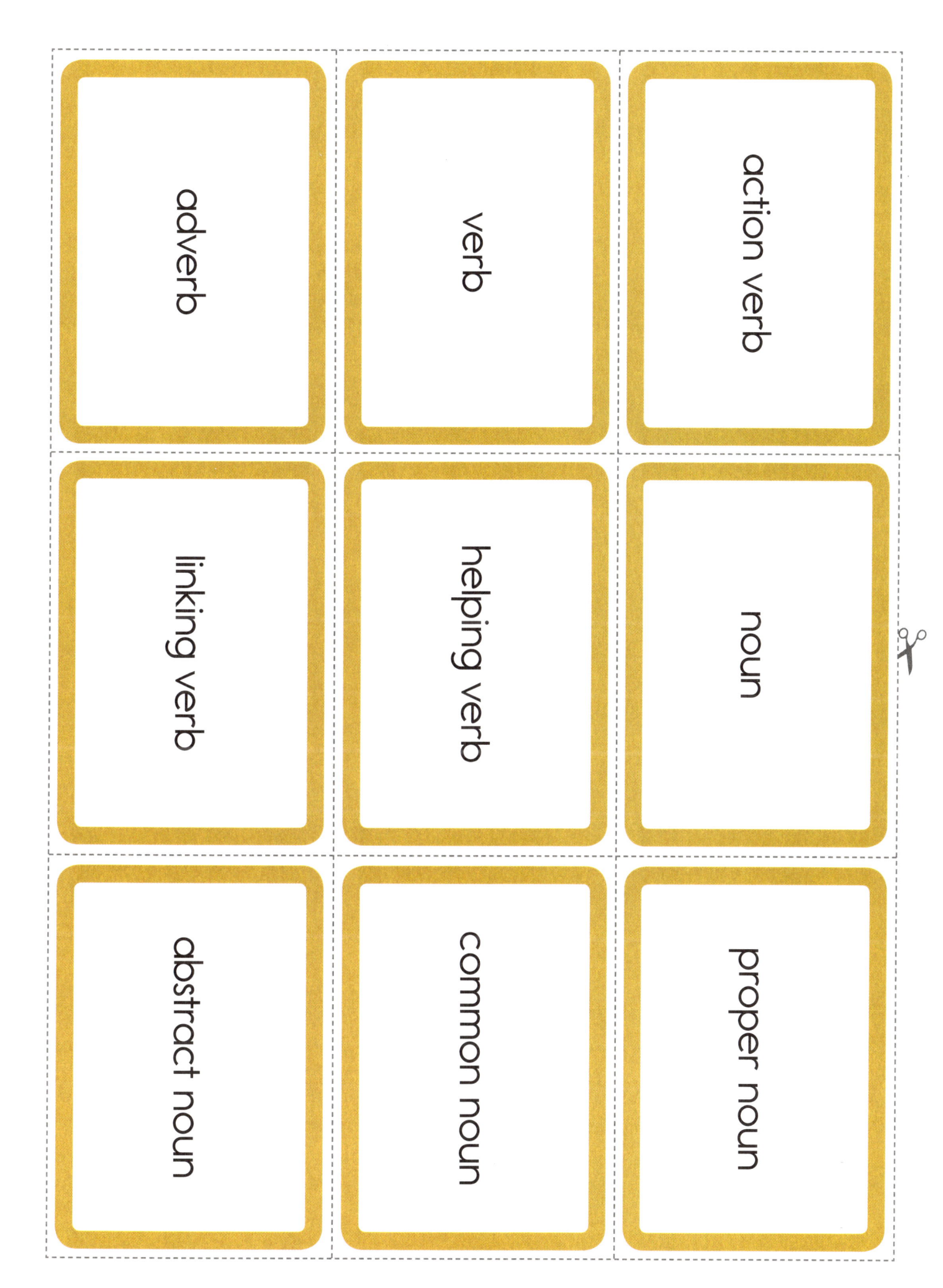

adverb	verb	action verb
linking verb	helping verb	noun
abstract noun	common noun	proper noun

a verb that tells what the noun is doing **run, jump, skip**	describes an action or state of being **run, feel**	describes a verb, adjective, or adverb **quickly, today, there, sometimes**
a person, place, or thing **baby, library, tree**	a verb that comes before the main verb **I will help.**	a verb that links a subject with its predicate **be, seem, feel**
a specific person, place, or thing **Mr. Ali, New York, October**	a general name for a person, place, or thing **teacher, ocean, holiday**	a feeling, a concept, or an idea **love, wisdom, friendship**

© Carson Dellosa

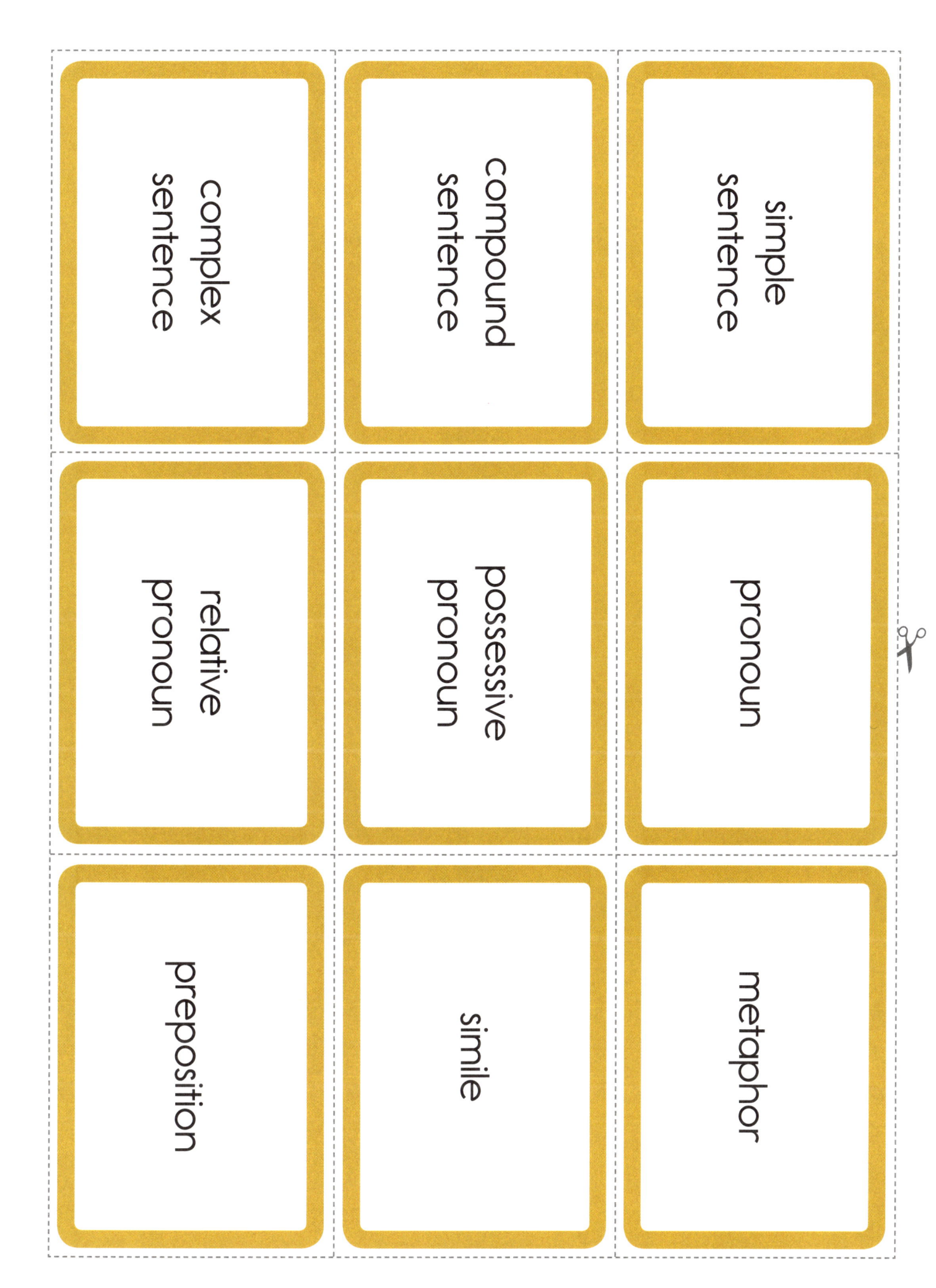

simple sentence	compound sentence	complex sentence
pronoun	possessive pronoun	relative pronoun
metaphor	simile	preposition

a sentence with one independent clause **I play soccer.**	a sentence with two or more independent clauses **Learning to play piano is hard, but I enjoy taking lessons.**	a sentence with one independent clause and at least one dependent clause **When I grow up, I want to be an astronaut.**
a word that takes the place of a noun **she, he, they, it**	a pronoun that shows ownership **mine, yours, theirs**	a pronoun that begins a phrase that describes a noun **who, that, which**
describing something by comparing it to something very different **Her hands were icicles when she woke up.**	describing something by comparing it to something very different with *like* or *as* **Her eyes were like a stormy sea.**	describes the relation of a noun or pronoun to other words in a sentence **with, on, in**

© Carson Dellosa

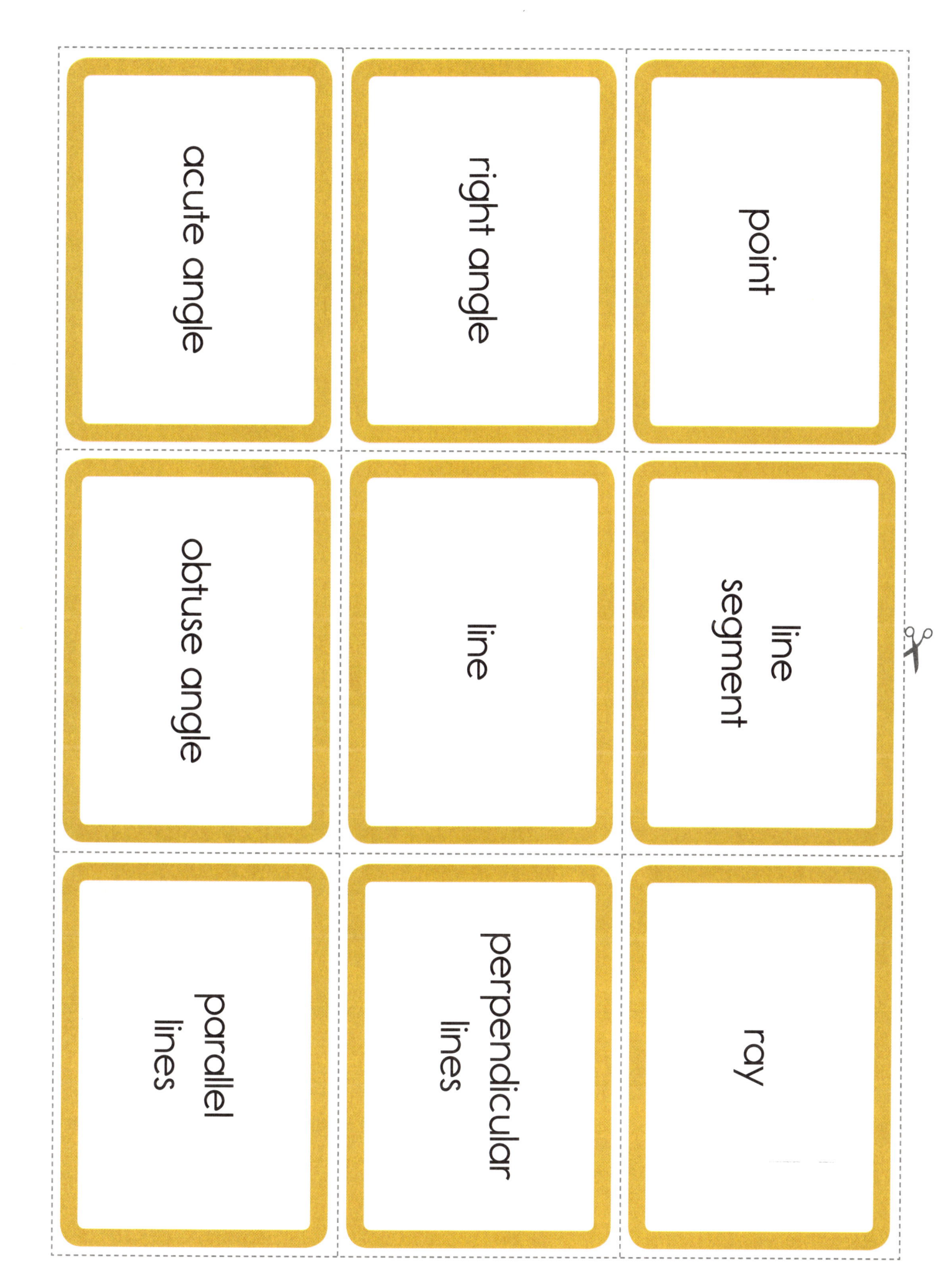

acute angle	right angle	point
obtuse angle	line	line segment
parallel lines	perpendicular lines	ray

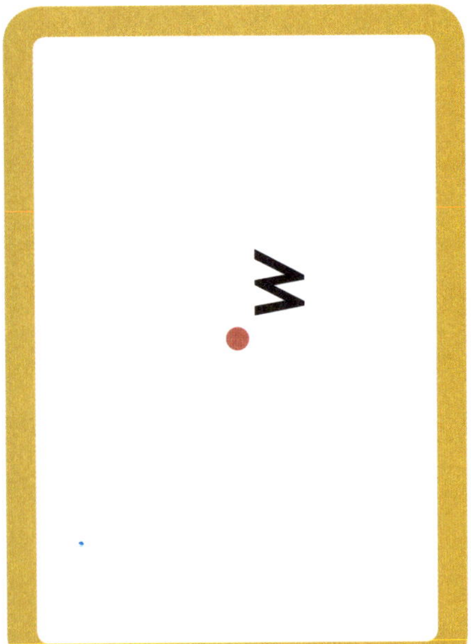
W

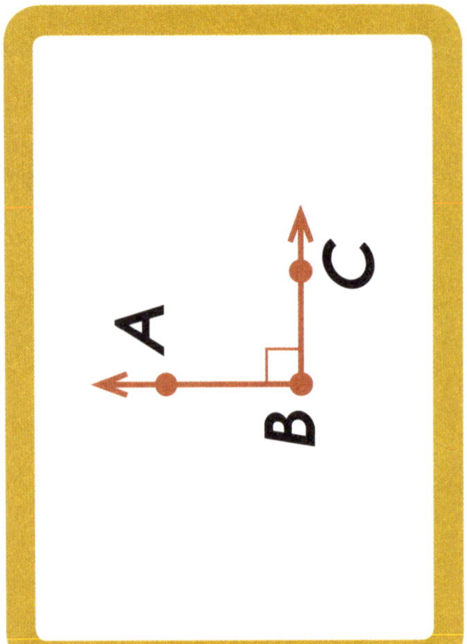
A
B
C

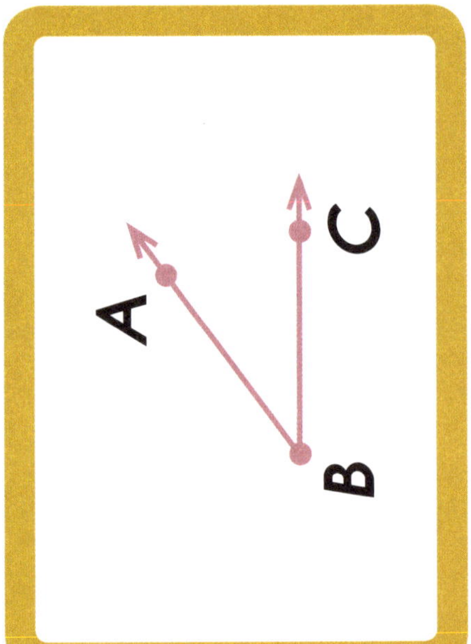
A
B
C

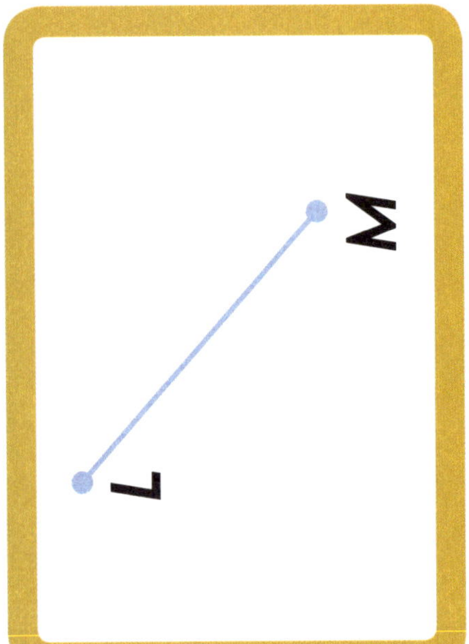
L
M

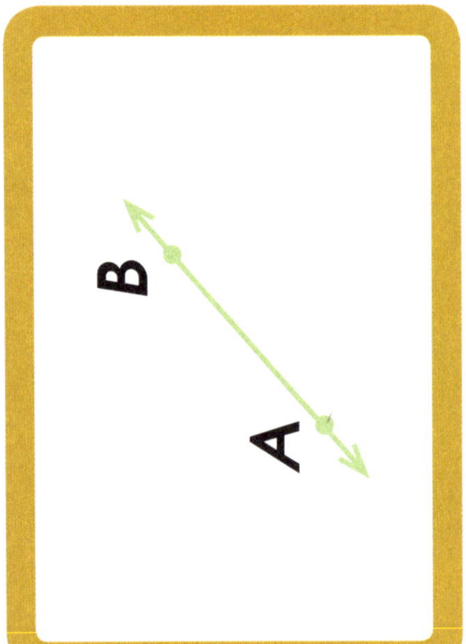
B
A

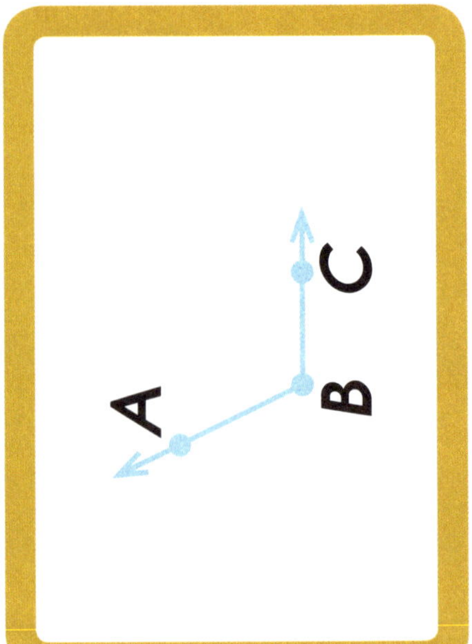
A
B
C

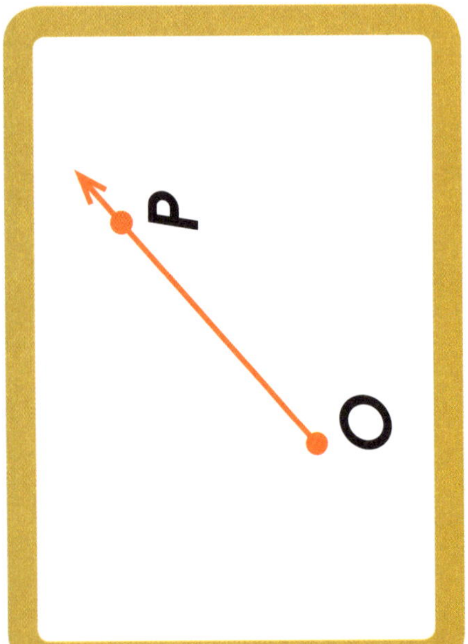
P
O

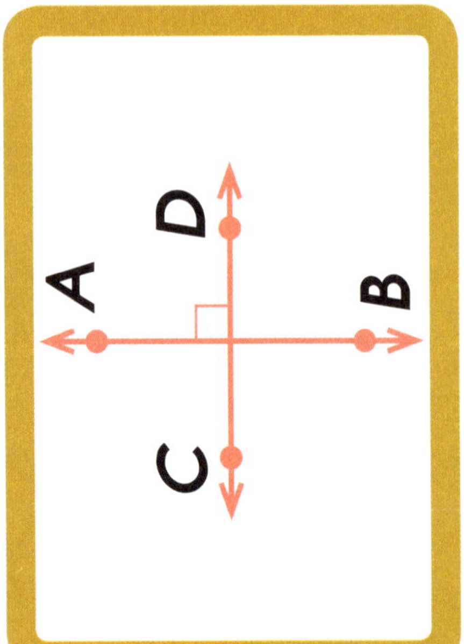
A
D
B
C

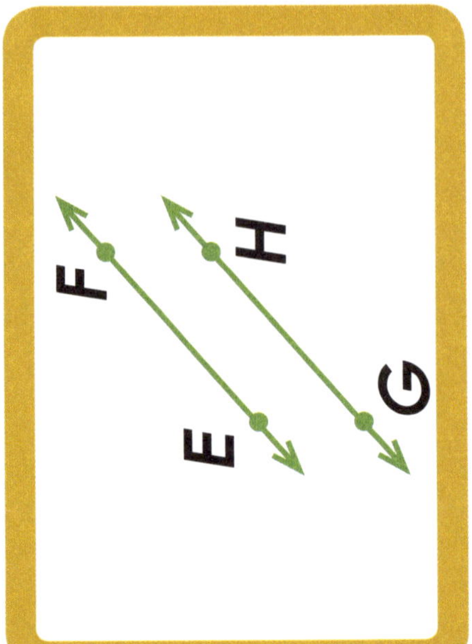
F
H
E
G

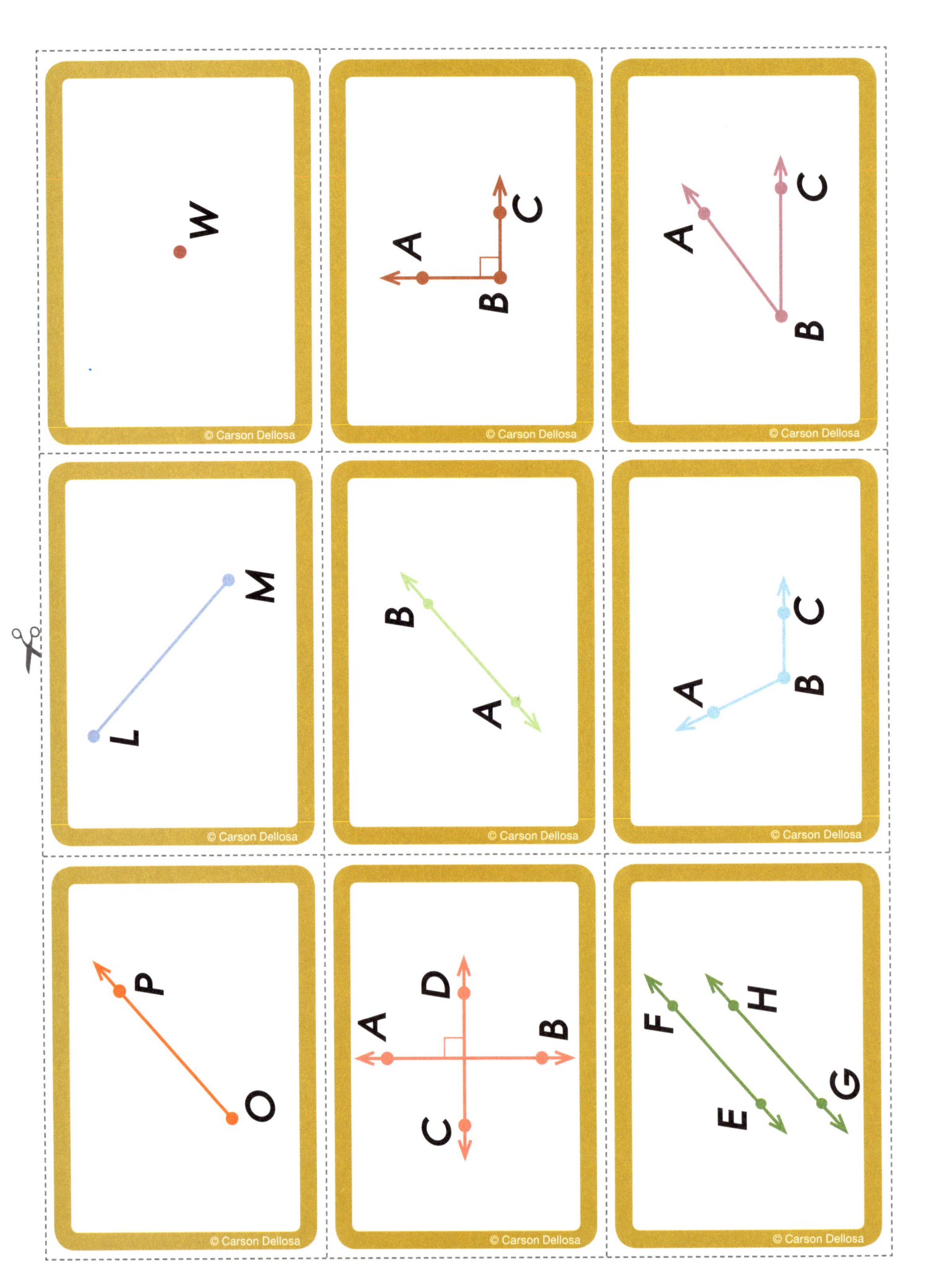

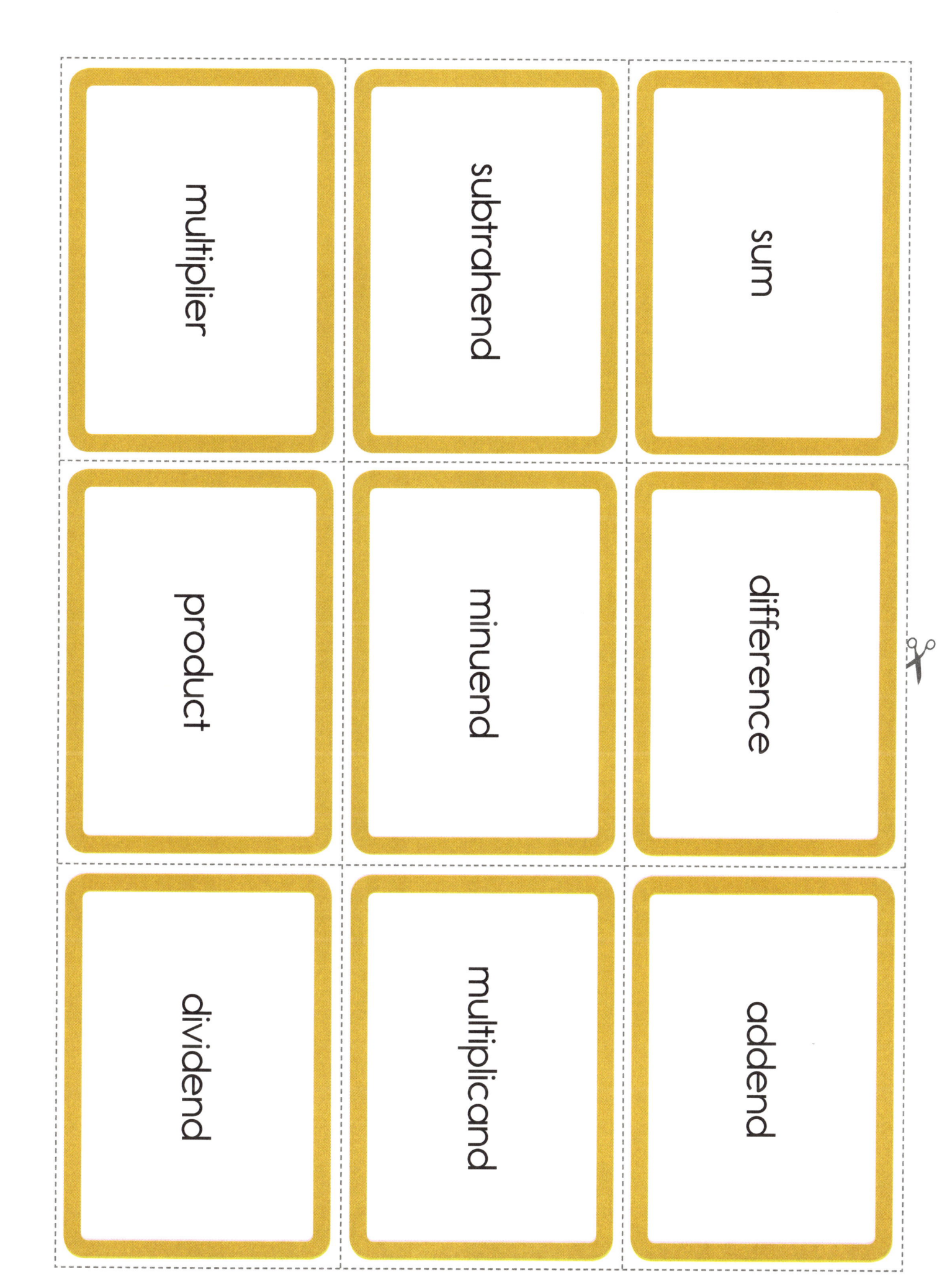

multiplier	subtrahend	sum
product	minuend	difference
dividend	multiplicand	addend

the total you get when you add two or more numbers 9 + 5 = 14	a number that is to be subtracted from another number 14 − 5 = 9	the number by which you multiply another 4 × 3 = 12 4 × 3 12
the answer to a subtraction problem 14 − 5 = 9	a number from which another number is to be subtracted 14 − 5 = 9	the answer to a multiplication problem 4 × 3 = 12 4 × 3 12
a number added to another number 9 + 5 = 14	a number that is to be multiplied by another number 4 × 3 = 12 4 × 3 12	the number that is divided 8 ÷ 2 = 4 4 2)8

© Carson Dellosa

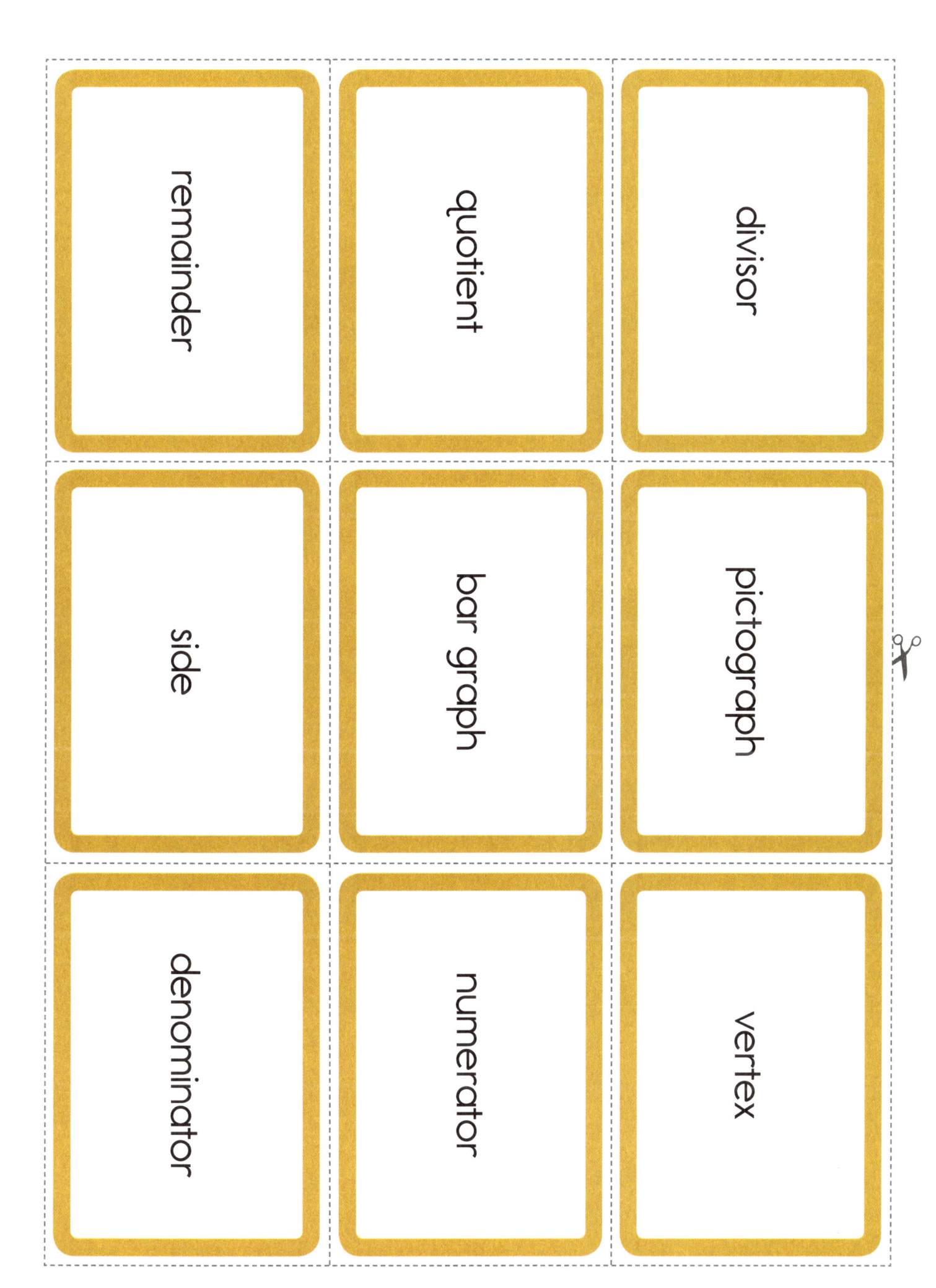

remainder	quotient	divisor
side	bar graph	pictograph
denominator	numerator	vertex

the number that you divide by

8 ÷ 2 = 4   4
            2)8

---

the answer in a division problem

8 ÷ 2 = 4   4
            2)8

---

the number left over when a number can't be divided evenly by another

7 ÷ 3 = 2 r1

---

a graph that shows information using picture symbols

---

a chart that compares information using rectangular bars

---

a straight line that is part of the boundary of a shape

---

a point on a shape where two or more edges meet

---

the number above the line in a fraction

$\frac{1}{2}$

---

the number below the line in a fraction

$\frac{1}{2}$

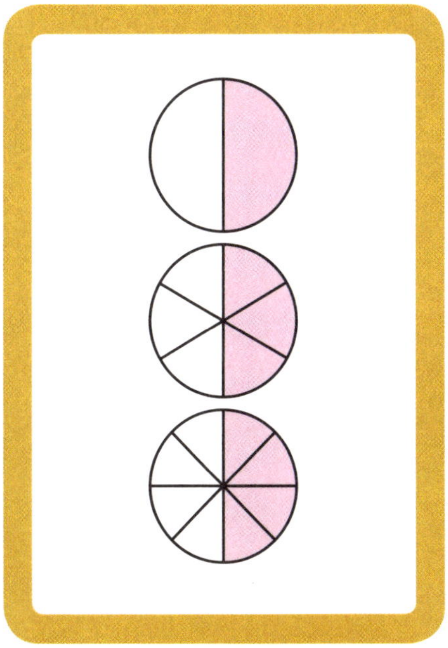
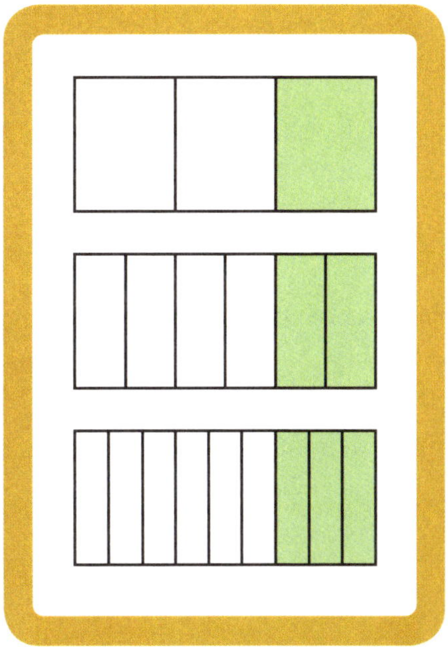
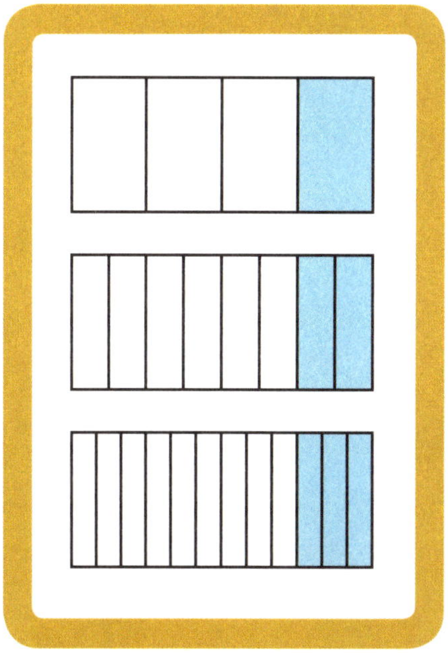
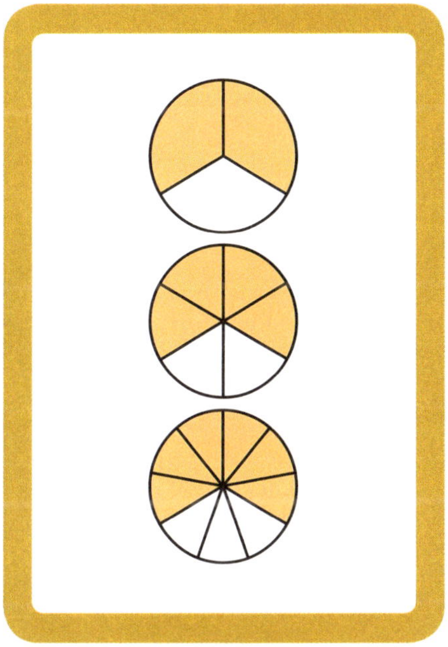
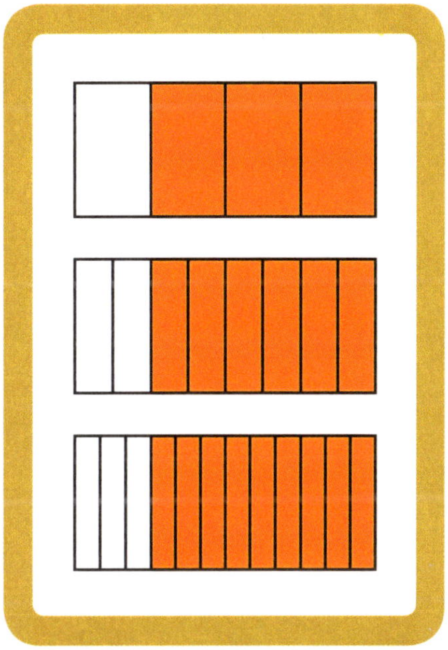
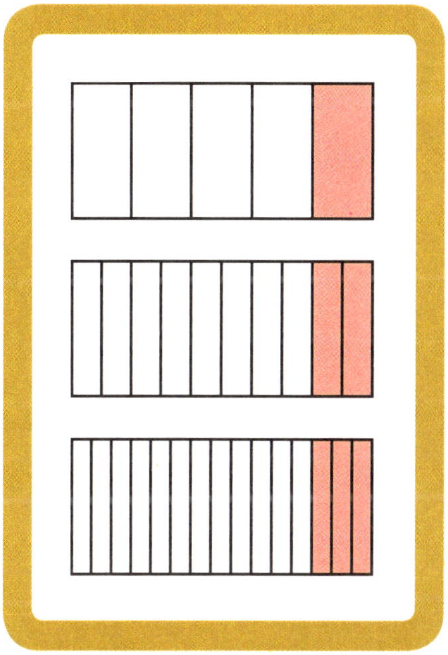
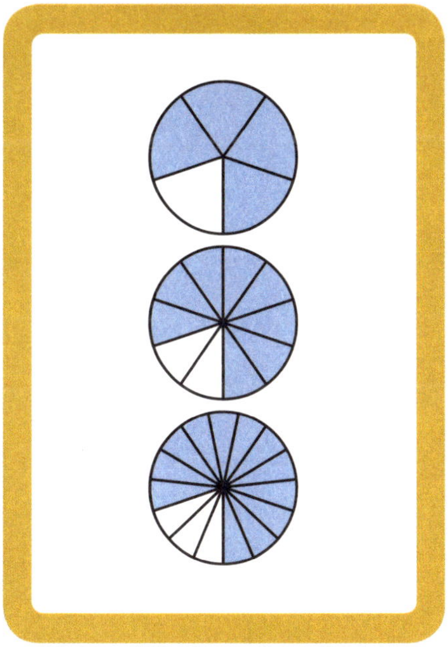
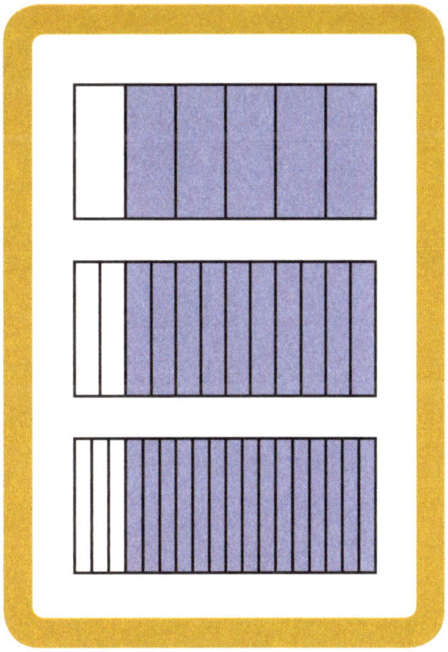
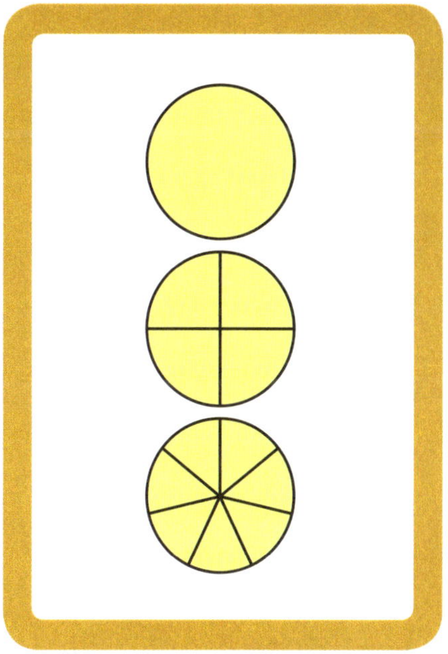

$\frac{1}{4} = \frac{2}{8} = \frac{3}{12}$	$\frac{1}{3} = \frac{2}{6} = \frac{3}{9}$	$\frac{1}{2} = \frac{3}{6} = \frac{4}{8}$
$\frac{1}{5} = \frac{2}{10} = \frac{3}{15}$	$\frac{3}{4} = \frac{6}{8} = \frac{9}{12}$	$\frac{2}{3} = \frac{4}{6} = \frac{6}{9}$
$1 = \frac{4}{4} = \frac{7}{7}$	$\frac{5}{6} = \frac{10}{12} = \frac{15}{18}$	$\frac{4}{5} = \frac{8}{10} = \frac{12}{15}$

My Third Grade to Fourth Grade
Progress Chart

Place a sticker on the path after you've completed each day.

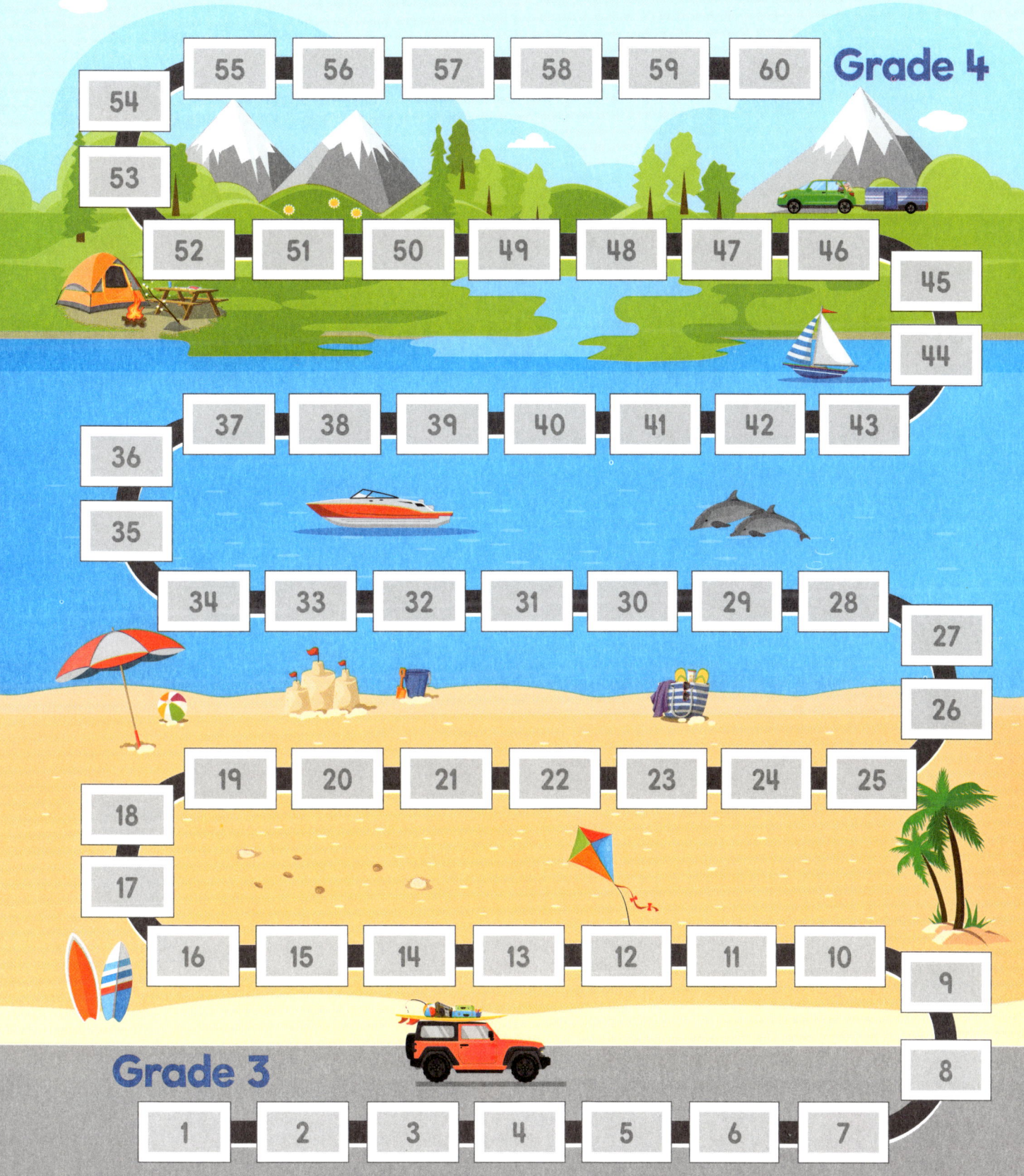

Grade 4

55 56 57 58 59 60
54
53
52 51 50 49 48 47 46
45
44
37 38 39 40 41 42 43
36
35
34 33 32 31 30 29 28
27
26
19 20 21 22 23 24 25
18
17
16 15 14 13 12 11 10
9
8

Grade 3

1 2 3 4 5 6 7

Reference Chart

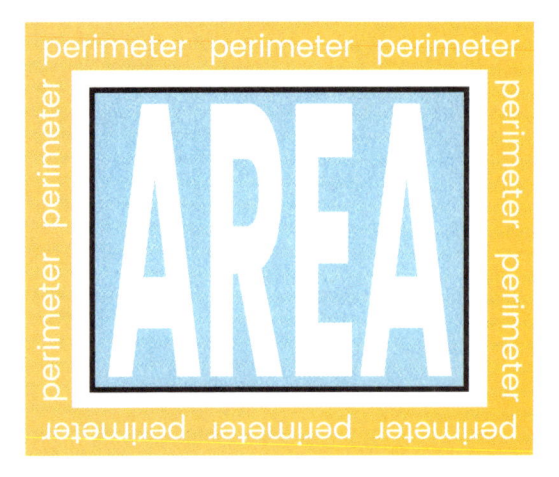

	AREA: The space (measured in square units) that a shape covers	**A = l × w** Count the squares or multiply the sides.
	PERIMETER: The distance around a shape	**P = side + side + side + side** **P = (2 × l) + (2 × w)** Add the sides together.
	**VOLUME:** The amount of space (measured in cubic units) inside a 3D figure	**V = length × width × height** **V = l × w × h** Count the cubic units.

G = gallon   Q = quart   P = pint   C = cup

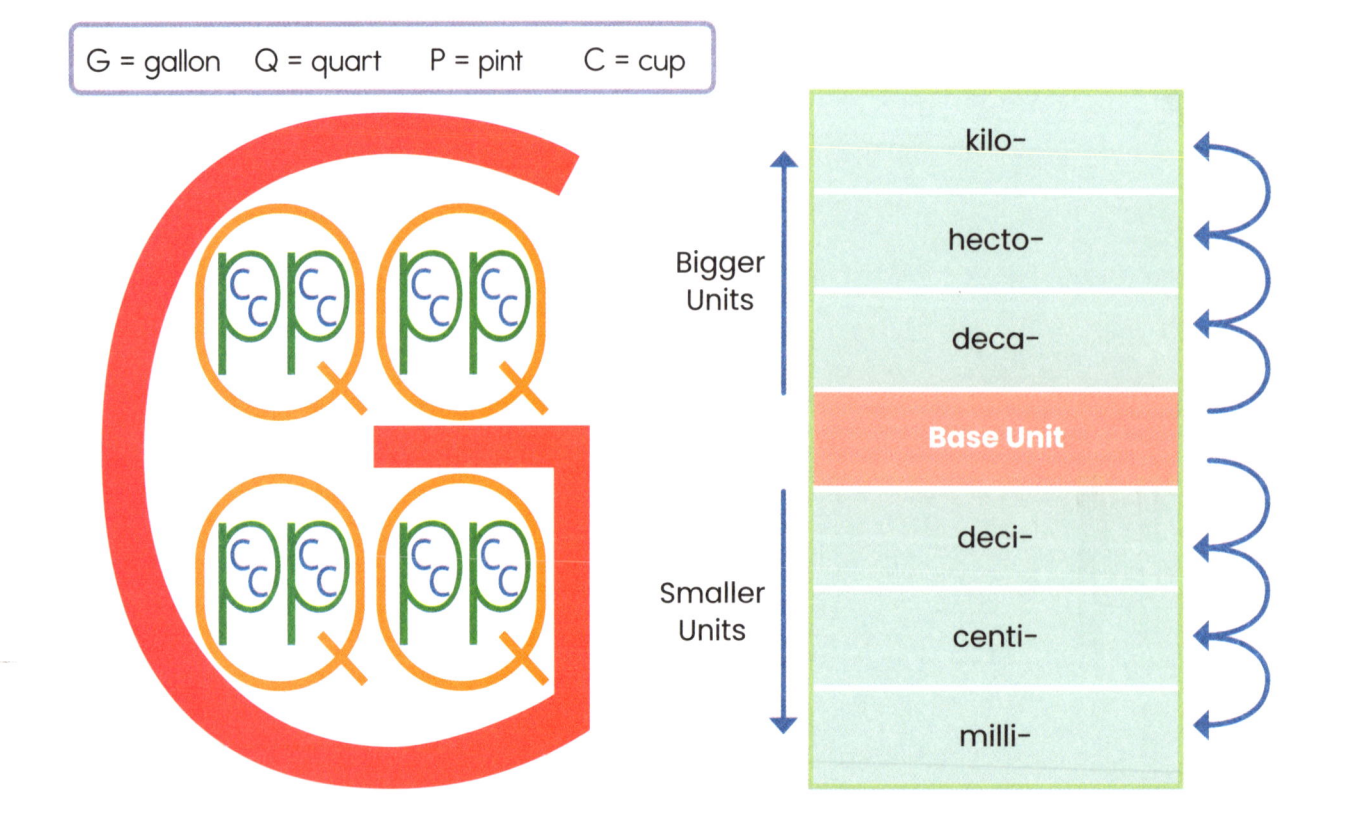

Bigger Units ↑	kilo-
	hecto-
	deca-
	Base Unit
Smaller Units ↓	deci-
	centi-
	milli-